I Should Have Been...

I SHOULD HAVE BEEN...

Phil Philcox

PHAROS BOOKS
A Scripps Howard Company
New York

First published in 1990.

Library of Congress
Cataloging-in-Publication Data

Philcox, Phil.
   I should have been / Phil Philcox.
      p.   cm.
   ISBN 0-88687-585-4: $6.95
   1. Employment tests—Humor.
   I. Title.
HF5549.5.E5P55   1990
153.9'4'00207—dc20   89-78537
                                              CIP

Interior design: Ruth Kolbert
Cover design: Nancy Carey

Printed in United States of America

Pharos Books
A Scripps Howard Company
200 Park Avenue
New York, NY 10166

10 9 8 7 6 5 4 3 2 1

Preface

This book would never have been written without the experts—those people who know a lot of things about a lot of subjects. The contributors range from college professors to private detectives, from owners of restaurants and schools to cooks and bomb disposal experts, from TV show producers to nonprofessionals who knocked on my door and offered to provide some challenging questions on their specialties. While the experts were making their contributions, I was thumbing through encyclopedias, almanacs, and books of all sorts looking for new subjects to challenge those who enjoy taking tests just for the fun of it. What I discovered in compiling this book was that knowledge isn't an exact science and that accepting the challenge of answering questions about something you know little or nothing about is—for most people—a heroic undertaking indeed. There are no scores as such in this book, but if you can answer about 50 percent of the questions on each quiz correctly, you're certainly a well-informed individual. If you can answer 70 percent or more correctly, you rank in the top 10 percent of the country's informed individuals. The worst that could happen is that your scores are low enough to verify the fact that you're probably more qualified to pursue the career you've already chosen in life than to make any drastic changes.

. . . and there's more to come. If you have any questions you would like to contribute to the next edition of this book, send them to Phil Philcox, c/o The Press Association, 1845 Main

Street, Newcomb, New York 12852 or fax your material to
518-582-3999. I'm particularly interested in career, general knowledge, and cultural tests that will challenge the readers. Multi-
ple choice with a few true-false thrown in is the preferred
format and length can range from ten to forty questions.
Please, don't forget the answers and include your name, ad-
dress, and daytime telephone number so we can contact you if
necessary. If we use your questions, we'll acknowledge you in
the book as one of our elite contributors.

PHIL PHILCOX
Newcomb, New York
November 1989

Acknowledgments

My thanks go to the following contributors: Joseph Alercia II, director of the Lion Investigation Academy in Bethlehem, Pennsylvania; Howie Barrow of the Howie Barrow Golf School in Grenelefe, Florida; Alan Caruba of the Boring Institute in New Jersey; Tzow-Chyi Chen of the Ming Court Restaurant in Orlando, Florida; Harold Cunningham of the Scientific Psychic's Association in Bowie, Texas; the staff at the Miss America Pageant in Atlantic City, New Jersey; Jim Hendricks and Rosalie M. Huerta of Prime Concepts, Inc., of Westport, Connecticut; the staff at King World in New York; the instructors at the Metropolitan Taxi Driver's School in London, England; John Weaver of Liberty Television and the staff at Orbis Communications; Dave Huntress, weatherman for WPTZ Television in Plattsburgh, New York; Renee Loosbrock, president of Guide Service of Washington in Washington, D.C.; Jeanine Drysdale Lowe, deputy sergeant at arms at the U.S. Senate in Washington; Pamela Matecat, Mark Davis, Chris Quilty, and Molly Stevens of the New England Culinary Institute in Montpelier, Vermont; Wendy McCabe of Robinson, Yesawich and Pepperdine, Inc., of Maitland, Florida; John Means of the National Association of Self-Instructional Language Programs at Temple University in Philadelphia, Pennsylvania; Tom Murphy of the Washington, D.C., Convention and Visitors Association; Glenn Petersen, assistant director of the U.S. Chess Federation in New Windsor, New York; Mary Sequin and Judy Menard of the Clinton-Essex-Franklin County Library System in upstate New York; Carl D.

Spurgeon, director of licensing for the American Motorcycle Foundation in Costa Mesa, California; Janice Sullivan of Dundee, New York; James J. Wade, vice president of corporate planning for The Nanny Institute of Beverly Hills and the Georgia School of Bartending in Atlanta, Georgia; George Walsh of Newcomb, New York; Donald Zeigler, associate professor of geography at Old Dominion University in Norfolk, Virginia; the staff at the Professional Golfers' Association in Palm Beach Gardens, Florida; the staff at the National Endowment of the Arts; Mike Gargiulo and the staff at Phoenix Communiocations Group in New York; the staff at Merv Griffin Enterprises in Hollywood, California; the personnel staff at the New York State Department of Civil Service and Corrections in Albany, New York; the Witches' League for Public Awareness in Salem, Massachusetts

A special thanks to Michael P. Rudman, editor-in-chief of National Learning Corporation. NLC published five thousand career examination preparation PASSBOOKS. Anyone taking any type of writtenexamination should contact NLC at 212 Michael Drive, Syosset, NY 11791 (516-921-8888 or 800-645-6337) for a test preparation book before taking their examination. These PASSBOOKS are highly recommended. Many of NLC's copyrighted tests are featured in this book and reprinted with permission.

Contents

☆ T H E ☆
WEATHERMAN
Test

Match the average cloud height with the cloud families listed below:

1. High with mean heights of 16,500 to 45,000 feet
   A. stratocumulus
   B. altostratus
   C. cirrostratus

2. Medium with heights of 6,500 to 23,000 feet
   A. nimbostratus
   B. cumulus
   C. cumulonimbus

3. Low with heights of 0 to 6,500 feet
   A. altocumulus
   B. altrostratus
   C. stratus

4. On the average, there are 19 to 25 typhoons in the _____ every year.
   A. South Atlantic
   B. North Atlantic
   C. Indian Ocean
   D. Western Pacific

5. On the average, there are five to eight hurricanes in the _____ every year.

1

A. Atlantic
B. Indian Ocean
C. Western Pacific
D. South Pacific

6. A sample of dry air contains by volume about:
    A. 78 percent nitrogen, 21 percent oxygen
    B. 78 percent oxygen, 21 percent nitrogen
    C. 32 percent argon, 57 percent mixed gases
    D. 57 percent carbon dioxide, 32 percent argon

7. You occasionally see a blue moon.
    True   False

8. "A closed atmospheric circulation rotating counterclock-
    wise in the Northern Hemisphere and clockwise in the
    Southern Hemisphere" best describes:
    A. a tropical disturbance
    B. a cyclone
    C. a hurricane
    D. typhoon

9. When hurricane conditions are expected within a 24-hour
    period, a hurricane warning is issued along coastal areas
    when the winds reach at least:
    A. 54 miles per hour
    B. 74 miles per hour
    C. 90 miles per hour
    D. 100 miles per hour

10. If the sky becomes overcast with cirrus and cirrostratus
    clouds, precipitation is likely.
    True   False

11. Officially, air frost occurs when the temperature of the air
    _____ feet above the ground falls below 0
    degrees C.
    A. 1,000 feet
    B. 500 feet

C. 90 feet
D. 4 feet

12. Barometers are usually calibrated in:
A. decimeters
B. millibars
C. degrees
D. isobars

13. Clouds form because the original cloud-free air is heated by water vapor and it evaporates and clings to the dust and salt particles in the air. If the temperature is low enough, ice particles are produced.
True   False

14. The principal cause of damage in most hurricanes is:
A. flooding
B. the rain
C. the wind
D. Both A and B are correct.

15. Radiation fog normally occurs only when the sun is overhead.
True   False

16. Drizzle differs from raindrops in that:
A. The water in drizzle has a higher temperature than the water in raindrops.
B. The droplets in drizzle are smaller than the droplets in raindrops.
C. There is no difference scientifically.
D. The raindrops come from clouds at a higher altitude than the clouds that produce drizzle.

17. One of the most important factors in determining fog conditions is:
A. the dew point spread
B. the drop in barometric pressure
C. the drop in temperature during a 12-hour period
D. the Altitude Scale Readings

☆ T H E ☆
DISTRICT ATTORNEY
Test

1. A person is always guilty of a felony if he unlawfully possesses:
   A. any loaded firearm in a vehicle
   B. any deadly weapon and is not a citizen of the United States
   C. any dagger or razor with intent to use the same unlawfully against another
   D. a shotgun in a building used for educational purposes

2. Intending to rob Smith of his watch, Jones knocks Smith to the ground without causing physical injury and demands to watch. Upon learning that Smith does not have the watch in his possession, Jones runs away. According to the penal law, which of the following best explains whether or not Jones is guilty of attempted robbery in the third degree?
   A. Jones is not guilty of an attempt since it was factually impossible for him to commit the robbery itself.
   B. Jones is guilty because he might have caused physical injury in the course of attempting the robbery.
   C. Jones is not guilty since Smith did not have the watch in his possession and Jones has an affirmative defense.
   D. Jones is guilty since he could have committed the robbery if the surrounding circumstances were what he thought them to be.

    E. Jones is not guilty because there is no evidence that Smith resisted Jones's demand for the watch.

3. Which of the following describes a person guilty of escape in the first degree?
   A. A person convicted of a felony escapes from a detention facility.
   B. A person just convicted of a misdemeanor escapes from a courtroom by impersonating a police officer.
   C. A person escapes from a police officer's custody by causing serious physical injury to the officer.
   D. After committing a felony, a person escapes from the scene of the crime by using or threatening the immediate use of a deadly weapon.

4. In cases of prostitution, complaints against offenders are drawn under the criminal procedure law because:
   A. Fines imposed for violations of this statute are payable into the city treasury rather than the state treasury.
   B. A heavier penalty is imposed for violations of that law than is imposed for violation of pertinent sections of the penal law.
   C. Under this law the testimony of the arresting officer as a matter of law does not require corroboration.
   D. Violations of pertinent sections of the penal law are offenses only, rather than crimes.

5. The police stop a car in which three men are riding. Ward is the driver and Jones and King are passengers. During a lawful search, the police find a quarter of an ounce of morphine concealed in King's coat. Based on these facts, it would be correct to state that:
   A. King, Jones, and Ward are all guilty of criminal possession of a dangerous drug.
   B. A presumption of knowingly possessing the morphine applies to Ward but not Jones.
   C. King is guilty of criminal possession of a dangerous drug and Ward is guilty of conspiracy.

D. King is guilty of criminal possession of a dangerous drug but Ward and Jones are not.

6. The category "malicious mischief" includes many different types of illegal acts of varying degrees of gravity. Which of the following acts of malicious mischief is considered a felony?
   A. the deliberate cutting of a telephone wire as a prank by college students
   B. the wanton destruction of fire extinguishers in a public building
   C. the malicious removal of a danger sign lawfully posted within a public highway
   D. the willful extinguishing of the light in a buoy lawfully placed in the waters within the state

7. Which of the following is hearsay?
   A. a written statement by a person not present at the court hearing where the statement is submitted as proof of an occurrence
   B. an oral statement in court by a witness of what he saw
   C. a written statement of what he saw by a witness present in the court
   D. a reenactment by a witness in court of what he saw

8. In a criminal case, a statement by a person not present in court is:
   A. acceptable evidence if not objected to by the prosecutor
   B. acceptable evidence if not objected to by the defense lawyer
   C. not acceptable evidence except in certain well-settled circumstances
   D. not acceptable evidence under any circumstances

9. Knowing that his friend, Jones, intends to rob a bank, Smith gives Jones a rifle to use during the robbery. The day before the robbery is supposed to occur, the police arrest Jones on an old charge, thereby preventing the

robbery. Based on these facts, it would be correct to state that Smith is:

A. not guilty of any crime
B. guilty of conspiracy in the second degree and criminal facilitation in the second degree
C. guilty of criminal facilitation in the second degree but not guilty of conspiracy in the second degree
D. guilty of conspiracy in the second degree but not guilty of criminal facilitation in the second degree

10. Each of the following statements refers to the use of force by a person other than a peace officer when that person reasonably believes such to be necessary to prevent the commission of an offense. According to the penal law, which of these statements is incorrect?

A. The person may use deadly physical force to prevent arson even if he is not an owner of the threatened premises or privileged to be thereon.
B. The person may use deadly physical force to prevent burglary of a dwelling if he is privileged to be in such dwelling.
C. The person may use physical force in order to prevent a crime involving damage to premises.
D. A person may use deadly physical force to prevent arson if he is in control of the threatened premises.
E. The person may use physical force to prevent criminal trespass, even if he is not an owner of the threatened premises or privileged to be thereon.

☆ THE ☆
FOOTBALL REFEREE
Test

1. Chucking is defined as:
   A. a violation of any playing rule
   B. warding off an opponent by contacting him with an extension of the arm
   C. touching of a loose ball by a player in an unsuccessful attempt to obtain possession
   D. a shift in the movement of two or more offensive players

2. The toss of the coin takes place:
   A. three minutes before the kickoff
   B. five minutes before the kickoff
   C. in the locker room an hour or more before kickoff
   D. anytime after both teams arrive at the stadium

3. The standard football playing field is 360 feet long and:
   A. 100 yards wide
   B. 160 yards wide
   C. 100 feet wide
   D. 160 feet wide

4. The home team in every game must provide _____ footballs to the referee.
   A. 10
   B. 14

C. 20
D. 24

5. Both hands extended overhead is the official signal for:
A. an illegal forward pass
B. a touchdown, field goal, or successful try
C. a delay of the game or excess time out
D. a dead ball

6. College football uses a crossbar 23 feet, 4 inches in length between the uprights. The NFL uses a crossbar that is:
A. the same length, only 8 inches higher from the ground
B. 18 feet, 6 inches
C. 22 feet, 6 inches
D. exactly 20 feet

7. The down indicator must:
A. be at least 4 feet high
B. be at least 5 feet high
C. be at least one foot over the referee's head
D. be made from oak or ash

8. A ball legally free kicked or snapped that continues in play until the down ends is called:
A. a free kick ball
B. a live ball
C. a touchback
D. a contact ball

9. The yardage chain is:
A. 6 yards long when fully extended
B. 8 yards long when fully extended
C. 10 yards long when fully extended
D. 12 yards long when fully extended

10. The football used in NFL play must:
A. be under 10 ounces in weight and inflated to an air pressure of over 15 pounds per square inch
B. be between 14 and 15 ounces in weight and inflated to

an air pressure of between 12.5 and 13.5 pounds per square inch
C. be no longer in circumference than 28.5 inches
D. be manufactured in the U.S.A.
E. Both B and C are correct.
F. Both A and C are correct.
G. Both A and D are correct.

11. Shoes and belts worn by referees must be:
A. all black
B. black and white
C. all white
D. either black or white and officially approved by the league

12. In 1959, how many professional teams were in operation in the NFL?
A. none
B. 6
C. 12
D. 15

13. During play a team's coach may move unrestricted in an area that:
A. extends the length of the sidelines
B. does not put him in the field of play
C. extends ten yards in both directions from the middle of the team's bench
D. extends ten yards in all directions from the team's bench

14. Referees are not allowed to cut their stirrups because:
A. They allow for a uniform height on the calf.
B. They are the property of the league.
C. They can be removed with snaps.
D. They would restrict the use of the socks approved for wear by the league.

★ THE ★ NANNY
Test

The term "nanny" has been around since the British introduced it in the early 1700s. Also known as a "nursery nurse," a nanny is an in-home child care provider, a caregiver, a nurturer, a nurse, a teacher, and companion. Generally, nannies are responsible for food preparation, clothing maintenance, and housework only as it applies to the children living in that home. There are several nanny schools around the United States and, in order to be accepted into the training program, applicants must be at least 18 years of age, provide the school with personal references, and earn a minimum score on school tests.

The following tests are samples of the test administered by the nanny schools.

1. Hyperactive children are characterized by:
   A. thoughtfulness
   B. remorsefulness
   C. forgetfulness
   D. tiredness

2. As a nanny, what can you do for a child having a grand mal seizure?
   A. attempt to waken the child
   B. tilt the child's head back

   C. restrain the child's movement
   D. begin CPR

3. When speaking to a hearing-impaired child, you should:
   A. exaggerate lip movements
   B. be near the child
   C. provide distractions
   D. avoid eye contact

4. What could you do to help a speech-impaired child?
   A. discourage singing
   B. encourage rhyming games
   C. avoid limitations and impersonations
   D. all of the above

5. If a baby pulls at his ears and cries all morning, he probably:
   A. is having a temper tantrum
   B. is upset you're not listening to him
   C. has an ear infection
   D. has an emotional disorder

6. What is the first thing to do if a child eats a house plant?
   A. have the child drink milk
   B. have the child vomit
   C. call the poison control center
   D. call the parents

7. What would you do for a burn that appears red and without blisters?
   A. call the doctor immediately
   B. hold the burn under cold water for two to three minutes
   C. notify the parents first
   D. nothing at all

8. If a child you are caring for is bitten by the family dog, you should:
   A. clean the wound with soap and water
   B. comfort the child

C. notify the parents

D. all of the above

9. If a four-year-old child is coughing and choking at the table, you should:
   A. start CPR
   B. allow the child to cough
   C. put the child on the floor
   D. administer the Heimlich maneuver

10. While feeding a three-month-old child, you notice the baby is turning blue and making no noise. You should:
    A. lower the baby's head supported by your knee
    B. raise the baby's head in a sitting position
    C. raise the baby's arms
    D. burp the baby on your shoulder

11. What would be the first thing to do if you saw smoke coming from under your door?
    A. feel the door
    B. open the door
    C. open the window
    D. lay face down on the floor

12. In evaluating a bathroom for safety, what would you look for?
    A. medication up high
    B. toilet seat locks
    C. skid mat in the tub
    D. all of the above

13. What can you do to ease your disappointment when you leave a family?
    A. think of all the negative things that happened to you
    B. avoid mourning
    C. keep in touch by calling or writing
    D. decide to remain with the family

☆ T H E ☆
ARMY COOK
Test

1. The number of times brown rice will increase in volume while cooking is:
   A. none
   B. two
   C. four
   D. six

2. When boiling green vegetables, the cover should be removed for a few moments at the beginning of the cooking in order to:
   A. allow vegetable acids to escape
   B. preserve flavor
   C. allow the steam to escape
   D. preserve the vitamin content

3. If Swiss steak is to be served, it's best to use:
   A. beef rib
   B. beef loin
   C. bottom round
   D. top sirloin

4. Egg whites whip most quickly at:
   A. 0 degrees F.
   B. 30 degrees F.
   C. 70 degrees F.
   D. 80 degrees F.

5. Before cooking, which of the following vegetables must be soaked in water?
   A. string beans
   B. Brussels sprouts
   C. turnips
   D. celery

6. The typical proportion of a thin cream sauce is:
   A. 1 tablespoon fat, 1 tablespoon flour, and 2 cups milk
   B. 2 tablespoons fat, 2 tablespoons flour, and 1 cup milk
   C. 1½ tablespoons fat, 1½ tablespoons flour, and 1 cup milk
   D. 1 tablespoon fat, 1½ tablespoons flour, and 1 cup milk

7. In order to use a standardized recipe for apple pie throughout the year, it would be best to use
   A. frozen apples
   B. fresh sliced apples
   C. fresh apples of the same variety
   D. canned apples of the same brand name and code

8. Which of the following fats have the highest smoking temperature:
   A. butter
   B. soybean oil
   C. hydrogenated oil
   D. olive oil

9. Which one of the following entrées offers the least variation in texture?
   A. turkey, cranberry sauce, fried golden brown potatoes, and peas
   B. chopped sirloin, mushroom gravy, french fried potatoes, and broccoli spears
   C. oven-fried chicken, baked potato, peas, carrots, and a salad
   D. meat loaf, mashed potatoes, creamed spinach, and white bread

10. Scraping and prerinsing of dishes before running them through the dishwashing machine is necessary to:

A. shorten the time of the washing process
B. reduce the amount of detergent needed
C. prevent blocking of the nozzles in the rinse arm of the machine
D. remove food particles which harden at the wash temperature

11. If a high bacteria count on the dishes is found in one of the serving units, it is least important to:
   A. check the wash and rinse temperature of the dishwashing machine
   B. check the technique used in scraping, prerinsing, washing, and rinsing dishes
   C. inspect the serving unit, including all equipment, for cleanliness
   D. arrange for a physical examination of every employee in the department

12. After the boiling temperature has been reached, the cooking time for frozen vegetables is:
   A. one-half of that required for fresh vegetables
   B. about twice that required for fresh vegetables
   C. one-fourth of that required for fresh vegetables
   D. the same as for canned vegetables

13. One cup of margarine weighs approximately:
   A. 1½ lb.
   B. 1 lb.
   C. ¾ lb.
   D. ¼ lb.

14. Whole dry milk is preferable to evaporated milk for use as a beverage chiefly because:
   A. It takes less time to prepare.
   B. It contains more vitamins.
   C. It can be made to look and taste like whole milk.
   D. It contains more calories

★ T H E ★
QUIZ SHOW
CONTESTANT
Test

On a leading TV game show, three contestants answer questions posed in the form of statements. The contestant must provide the answer in the form of a question. Example: Question—Ridges, whorls, and phalanx. Answer—What are parts of a fingerprint?

In the first segment six categories—each with five questions ranging from $100 to $500—are presented. In the second segment six new categories—each with five questions ranging from $200 to $1,000—are presented. When all of the questions have been answered or time runs out, the contestants bet all or part of their winnings on one final question which could be on any subject. The winner is the contestant with the highest winnings.

Try the following questions to see how you can do. The first word of the answer is included to assist you in forming your question-answer.

Category—Islands

$100
1. St. Croix, St. John, and St. Thomas
    What _____?

$200
2. Adak, Amchitka, Attu, Kanaga, Kiska, Tanaga, Unmak, Unalaska, and Unimak
What _____?

$300
3. 840,000 square miles in area and a possession of Denmark
What _____?

$400
4. Guernsey, Jersey, and Sark
What _____?

$500
5. Leyte, Luzon, Mindanao, Mindoro, Negros, Palawan, Panay, and Samar
What _____?

Category—Seeing I To I
(All answers begin with the letter "I")

$100
6. Sardinia, Trieste, Lido, and the Isle of Caprera
What _____?

$200
7. Sun Valley, Boise, Hells Canyon, and the River of No Return.
What _____?

$300
8. An Indian word meaning "one who puts to sleep" or "beautiful land."
What _____?

$400
9. $53.9 million in 1987
What _____?

$500
10. An Islamic republic with a population of 51 million people
    speaking Persian, Turk, Kurdish, Arabic, and French.
    What _____?

Category—I-Synonyms
(All of the answers begin with the letter "I")

$100
11. Cerebral, bright, analytical, perceptive, advanced,
    promising
    What _____?

$200
12. Unresponsive, repressed, cold, restrained, reticent
    What _____?

$300
13. Inconclusive, illogical, unverified, unsure, hesitant
    What _____?

$400
14. Careless, undependable, untrustworthy, reckless, short-
    sighted
    What _____?

$500
15. Animate, inflame, encourage, and exhilarate
    What _____?

Category—State Governors

$100
16. Mario Cuomo
    Who _____?

$200
17. George Deukmejian
    Who _____?

$300
18. Madeleine Kunin
    Who _____?

$400
19. John Waihee
    Who _____?

$500
20. James R. Thompson
    Who _____?

Category—Personality Birthplaces

$100
21. London, England, May 29, 1903
  • Who _____?

$200
22. Liverpool, England, July 7, 1940
    Who _____?

$300
23. Tokyo, Japan, October 22, 1917
    Who _____?

$400
24. Tampico, Illinois, February 6, 1911
    Who _____?

$500
25. Gary, Indiana, August 29, 1958
    Who _____?

Category—From The Heart

$100
26. Approximately 4,000 Americans
    How many _____?

$200
27. Myocardial infarction
    What _____?

$300
28. December 3, 1967 in Capetown, South Africa
    When _____?

$400
29. Mary Martin hit
    What _____?

$500
30. The Heartbeat of America
    What _____?

Second Challenge

Category—B-Homonyms
(All of the answers start with the letter "B")

$200
31. Superior and one who gambles
    What _____?

$400
32. A telescope and a compass box
    What _____?

$600
33. An animal, to carry, and undressed
    What _____?

$800
34. A floating signal and a male child
    What _____?

$1,000
35. Timber and restless
    What _____?

Category—Chess

$200
36. 64
    How _____?

$400
37. 32
    How _____?

$600
38. Always white
    Who _____?

$800
39. Bobby Fischer, Joel Benjamin, Yasser Seirawan, and Walter Browne
    Who _____?

$1,000
40. The governing body of the world chess movement.
    What _____?

Category—Lakes, Rivers and Oceans

$200
41. 35,840 feet
    What _____?

$400
42. 3,710 miles
    What _____?

$600
43. HOMES
What _____?

$800
44. The Pacific Ocean, the Atlantic Ocean, the Indian Ocean,
the Arctic Ocean, and South China Sea.
What _____?

$1,000
45. From San Juan County, Colorado, to the Gulf of Mexico
What _____?

Category—Academy Awards
*(Name the actor, actress, or director who won the Academy
Award for the picture listed)*

$200
46. The French Connection
Who is _____?

$400
47. Coming Home
Who is _____?

$600
48. Kramer vs. Kramer
Who is _____?

$800
49. Lawrence of Arabia
Who is _____?

$1,000
50. Cabaret
Who is _____?

Category—Halls of Fame

$200
51. Fort Lauderdale, Florida
    Where _____?

$400
52. Cooperstown, New York
    Where _____?

$600
53. Stillwater, Oklahoma
    Where _____?

$800
54. Oklahoma City, Oklahoma
    Where _____?
    Fame?

$1,000
55. St. Louis, Missouri
    Where _____?

★ T H E ★
SHEPHERD
Test

1. You can determine a sheep's age fairly accurately by its teeth but only up to about age four. This is because:
   A. By age four, half of a sheep's teeth have fallen out and will not be replaced.
   B. By age four the sheep has all of its permanent teeth.
   C. The teeth are so worn down by age four that they are no longer a good indication of age.
   D. By age four, most sheep have no teeth.

2. The side-to-side pendulum motion a sheepdog makes while pushing stock forward and keeping them in a group is known as:
   A. breaking
   B. cuffing
   C. wearing
   D. close running

3. Dorset Horn sheep differ from most sheep in that:
   A. Both the ewe and ram have horns.
   B. Their wool is always black.
   C. Their fleece is very dense.
   D. They are the largest sheep bred in the United States.

4. In populated areas in the United States, dogs are a major threat to sheep. At last count, there were about:
   A. two dogs for every five sheep

   B. three dogs for every sheep
   C. an equal number of dogs and sheep
   D. five sheep for every dog

5. Barley as a feed grain is not recommended for sheep
   because:
   A. It stores poorly.
   B. It cannot be left out in the open.
   C. It causes metabolic disturbances in pregnant sheep.
   D. Too much barley in the diet causes the sheep's coat to
      dull.

6. The Great Pyrenees sheepdog is believed to have been an
   offspring of:
   A. the Kuvasz sheepdogs of Hungary
   B. the Maremma sheepdogs of Italy
   C. the Saint Bernard
   D. the Anatolian sheepdog of Turkey

7. During the breeding season, a ram's semen can be seri-
   ously damaged if the air temperature exceeds:
   A. 65 degrees F.
   B. 90 degrees F.
   C. 100 degrees F.
   D. any temperature under the ram's normal body tem-
      perature

8. In one breeding session, a healthy ram can service a
   maximum of:
   A. 2 to 4 ewes
   B. 4 to 6 ewes
   C. 10 to 15 ewes
   D. 25 to 30 ewes

9. The Old English Sheepdog is considered to be the best
   working dog available.
   True   False

10. Trimming the wool from around the crotch and udder
    before lambing is called:

A. waxing
B. facing
C. tagging
D. hipping

11. Sheep of most breeds are born with long tails.
    True   False

12. When docking or removing a sheep's tail:
    A. A sharp knife is the best tool because it provides a clean cut.
    B. A dull knife is the best tool because it causes less bleeding.
    C. It's best to use a general anesthetic.
    D. It's best to do it when the sheep is about six months old.

13. The meat from uncastrated males is usually:
    A. tougher than the meat from castrated males
    B. tougher than the meat from ewes
    C. more tender than the meat from castrated males
    D. the same as the meat from castrated males

14. Orphan lambs are called:
    A. doggies
    B. fosters
    C. newborns
    D. bummers

15. The best way to administer artificial respiration to a lamb is by blowing into its mouth.
    True   False

16. Next to starvation, pneumonia is probably the major cause of lamb deaths in the United States.
    True   False

☆ T H E ☆
CRIMINAL
INVESTIGATOR
Test

1. If several witnesses describing the same occurrence agree on most details, the investigator should then:
   A. determine whether or not these witnesses were in communication with each other
   B. assume that such agreement means that the recollection was true
   C. assume that the witnesses' observations were incorrect since two or more people usually will not agree on the same details
   D. question the witnesses again, concentrating on the details on which they differ

2. Of the following, the strongest indication that the signature on an important document is a forgery is that the suspected signature:
   A. is partially illegible
   B. shows a noticeable trembling in certain letters
   C. shows that the writer retouched several letters
   D. is identical in all respects with a signature known to be genuine

3. Experienced investigators have found that using the question-and-answer method in interviewing a witness, instead of allowing the witness to tell his own story freely and without interruption, most often tends to:

A. increase both the scope and the accuracy of the information given by the witness
B. increase the scope but decrease the accuracy of the information given by the witness
C. decrease both the scope and the accuracy of the information given by the witness
D. decrease the scope but increase the accuracy of the information given by the witness

4. Witnesses are usually most willing to discuss an event when they are:
   A. disinterested in the subsequent investigation
   B. interviewed immediately following the event
   C. interviewed for the first time
   D. known by the investigator

5. During the course of a routine interview, the best tone of voice for an interviewer to use is:
   A. authoritative
   B. uncertain
   C. formal
   D. conversational

6. Two witnesses were suspected of collusion. In this sentence, the word "collusion" means most nearly:
   A. a conflict of interest
   B. an unintentional error
   C. an illegal secret agreement
   D. financial irregularities

7. In his report, the investigator described several covert business transactions. In this sentence, the word "covert" means most nearly:
   A. unauthorized
   B. joint
   C. complicated
   D. secret

8. If an investigator receives an anonymous phone call from

a person claiming to have knowledge of criminal behavior in an agency that is currently being investigated, the investigator should:

    A. listen politely and make notes on the important facts given by the informant

    B. tell the informant what has already been discovered and ask if he has anything to add

    C. question the informant to obtain all of the information he has

    D. ask the informant to submit his information in writing

9. The first three digits of a Social Security number are coded for:

    A. the age of the cardholder when the card was issued

    B. the cardholder's initials

    C. the year the card was issued

    D. the area in which the card was issued

10. During an interview, a subject makes statements an investigator knows are false. Of the following, it would be most appropriate for the investigator to:

    A. point out each inconsistency in the subject's story as soon as the investigator detects it

    B. interrupt the subject and request that he submit to a polygraph test

    C. allow the subject to continue talking until he becomes enmeshed in his lies and then confront him with his falsehoods

    D. allow the subject to finish what he has to say and then implicitly inform him it is a crime to lie to an investigator

11. You are checking someone's work history. The best way to get the most reliable information from a previous employer is to:

    A. Send personal letters. The employer will respond to the personal attention.

    B. Send form letters. The employer will cooperate readily since little time or effort is asked of him.

    C. Arrange a personal interview. The employer may offer

information he would not care to put in a letter or discuss over the phone.
D. Telephone. This method is as effective as a personal interview and is much more convenient.

12. Assume that an investigator must, in the course of an investigation, question several people who know each other. To gather them all in one group and question them together is generally:
   A. a good practice since any inaccurate information offered by one person would be corrected by others in the group
   B. a poor practice since people in the group rarely pay adequate attention to questions
   C. a good practice since the investigator will save much time and effort in this way
   D. a poor practice since the presence of several people can inhibit an individual from speaking

13. During an important interview, an investigator takes notes from time to time but very rarely looks at the subject being questioned. Such action on the part of the investigator is:
   A. unacceptable, chiefly because during the actual interview an investigator should pay more attention to the witness's manner of giving the information rather than in the content of his statements
   B. acceptable, chiefly because data should be recorded at the earliest opportunity and important data should be noted meticulously
   C. unacceptable, chiefly because it inhibits the person being interviewed and is not conducive to a give-and-take discussion
   D. acceptable, chiefly because focusing attention on note-taking and not on the person being interviewed creates an impression of professional objectivity

☆ T H E ☆
SHIP'S OFFICER
AND DECKHAND
—————— *Test* ——————

1. The ship's beam is:
   A. the narrowest part of the ship
   B. the width of the ship at its widest point
   C. the length of the ship
   D. the height of the tallest mast on the ship

2. A Pitot tube is used:
   A. to determine a ship's speed
   B. to feed air into engines below deck
   C. to feed water into the water-cooled engines below deck
   D. to determine wind direction

3. The windward side of a ship is:
   A. the side exposed to the wind
   B. the side protected from the wind
   C. the east side when the ship is heading in a northerly direction
   D. the west side when the ship is heading in a northerly direction

4. A fathom is:
   A. a unit of depth or length measurement equal to 6 feet
   B. a unit of measurement equal to 36 feet
   C. the lowest deck on the ship
   D. The main corridor in the boiler room

5. The ship's bow is located:
   A. in the front of the ship
   B. in the back of the ship
   C. on the left or right side of the ship
   D. on the deck immediately forward of the main keel

6. The marine 24-hour day is usually divided into:
   A. 4 watches
   B. 6 watches
   C. 8 watches
   D. 12 watches

7. A ship's scuppers are:
   A. deckhands with little or no sea experience
   B. drains below the ship's rails
   C. deck openings with ladders leading to the lower decks
   D. experienced seamen

8. Dead reckoning is a common form of ship navigation. It means:
   A. locating a destination point using a sextant, the stars, and a topographic map
   B. heading in one direction without veering right or left
   C. the determination of the ship's position by keeping track of the distance and direction traveled
   D. the ability to locate a set point on the water by navigating by the stars

9. Sounding is:
   A. a procedure used to test hull strength
   B. a procedure used to test the depth of the water
   C. a procedure used to call passengers to dinner
   D. a procedure using a bell to denote the time of day

10. The Rules of the Road at Sea recognized by all countries pertain to:
    A. only ships over 300 feet in length
    B. any type of watercraft, including seaplanes

C. any type of watercraft operating in international waters
D. Both A and C are correct.

11. A league is:
    A. one nautical mile
    B. two nautical miles
    C. three nautical miles
    D. four nautical miles

12. A companionway is:
    A. a deck passengers use to congregate with friends
    B. a ladder or flight of stairs
    C. a recreation room, usually located on the main deck
    D. the main corridor leading to cabins

13. A marine sextant is used to:
    A. determine the location of the Big Dipper and the North Star
    B. measure the altitude of a heavenly body above the visible horizon
    C. locate stars in the sky
    D. focus in on a point on the horizon for the purpose of navigation

14. The ship's bridge is:
    A. the navigational center of the ship
    B. the deck containing the swimming pool
    C. the stairs leading to the uppermost deck
    D. the stairs leading to the lowermost deck

15. The bulkhead on a ship is:
    A. the main storage area for food supplies
    B. the walls separating enclosed areas
    C. the ceiling in any area of the ship
    D. the floor in any area of the ship

★ T H E ★
HOSPITAL NUTRITIONIST
Test

1. Obesity is a form of malnutrition.
   True   False

2. A pound of butter contains the equivalent number of calories as a pound of fat on your body.
   True   False

3. Obesity is often inherited.
   True   False

4. Crash diets are safe.
   True   False

5. Pizza is not a nutritious snack food.
   True   False

6. Of the following groups, the one which may be served on a soft diet is:
   A. cream soup, mashed potatoes, spinach puree, toast, butter, and custard
   B. broiled chicken, mashed potatoes, buttered peas, toast, and milk
   C. vegetable soup, lamb chops, mashed potatoes, lettuce, salad, and toast
   D. clear broth, baked potato, tenderloin steak, carrots, and apple pie

7. Sugar refined from sugar cane and sugar from sugar beets are the same.
   True   False

8. Women require more iron than men.
   True   False

9. Exercise is not necessary for small children.
   True   False

10. The increasing practice of eating out has had a marked effect on eating habits and obesity.
    True   False

11. You can never take too many vitamins and minerals.
    True   False

12. Water is important in the daily intake of the body chiefly because:
    A. It causes the oxidation of food in the body.
    B. It is a transporting medium for all body substances.
    C. It cools the air in the lungs.
    D. It gives off minerals when it is digested.

13. Of the following statements with respect to the nutritional needs of children, the one which is most accurate states:
    A. A child of four years of age requires a minimum of 2,000 calories a day.
    B. It is better for a child to be slightly underweight than to be overweight.
    C. Proportionately, children require more protein per pound of body weight than adults.
    D. A child whose diet is deficient in Vitamin D may develop scurvy.

14. Cholesterol occurs most abundantly in:
    A. peaches, cream, and carrots
    B. cream, cottonseed oil, and liver

C. cream, liver, and egg yolk
D. liver, carrots, and egg yolk

15. In trying to control calories, a 13-year old girl substitutes sweets for adequate amounts of milk, eggs, bread, potatoes, and vegetables. Her diet is most likely to be deficient in:
   A. calories, calcium, and carbohydrates
   B. calories, protein, and calcium
   C. protein, calcium, and iron
   D. protein, carbohydrates, and iron

16. Which of the following group of vegetables should be included in a reducing diet:
   A. Potatoes, lima beans, and okra
   B. Corn, beets, and broccoli
   C. Asparagus, broccoli, and cauliflower
   D. Carrots, baked beans, and parsnips

☆ T H E ☆
WITCH
— *Test* —

The art of being a witch is probably best defined as having supernatural powers for evil purposes if you're a black witch and the power to do good if you're a white witch. Most witches of note were women but there are a handful of male witches, often referred to as wizards or sorcerers. While the term "warlock" is often used, it is not recognized by most covens in the United States.

In order to practice one's witching skills, chants and spells are uttered, often over possessions of the victims. These spells, along with magic potions, powders, and other rituals bring about the desired results.

1. The chicken oracle ritual is used to determine the truth. A chicken is fed benge, a substance made from a poisonous vine. The practitioner speaks to the benge, telling it to kill the chicken if the statement was true. If the chicken dies, the next step is to:
    A. duplicate the ritual with a second chicken for definite results
    B. burn the chicken's feathers
    C. put the chicken's feathers in a cloth bag and place it around the neck of the truth seeker
    D. cut the chicken's feet off and toss them over your right shoulder

2. Giving a subject a live spider or caterpillar to wear like jewelry is used to:
   A. remove birthmarks
   B. cure whooping cough
   C. mend broken bones
   D. remove spells

3. The major ingredients of magic flying ointment are:
   A. wolfsbane, aconite, hemlock, poplar leaves, and bat's blood
   B. the feathers and blood of any flying animal
   C. ground bark from high up in trees
   D. bat's blood, owl's blood, and crow's blood mixed with garlic, hemlock, and wolfsbane

4. Making a heap of wheat or grain in a place where a person has died is used to:
   A. prevent other people from dying of the same disease
   B. prevent only other family members from dying of the same disease
   C. permit the sun to shine again on that spot
   D. create a sacred place free from intrusion by evil spirits

5. Trimming a person's hair and nails and putting the trimmings under the bed along with a dead rooster has always been a sure cure for:
   A. insanity
   B. leprosy
   C. epilepsy
   D. gout

6. A subject is suffering from severe arthritis. One cure used by thirteenth-century practitioners was to:
   A. rub the patient's forehead with pieces of toad
   B. bury the patient in a graveyard for a minimum of two hours
   C. plant wolfsbane around the patient's house
   D. boil the patient in hot oil

7. One of the dangers of digging up mandrakes is that the shrieking of the disturbed plants has been known to drive the digger insane. A popular solution to this problem is:
   A. send dogs to do it
   B. dig up the roots with your hands behind your back
   C. sprinkle your hands with garlic before digging
   D. stab the roots with a silver blade to stop the shrieking

8. Sabbat is:
   A. a amulet or talisman
   B. the name of a fourteenth-century witch in Europe
   C. a potion used to make witches fly
   D. the witches' Sabbath

9. May 1 is considered to be:
   A. the beginning of sacrifice week
   B. the day of a Druidic feast called Beltane
   C. the festival of corpses
   D. Walpurgis Night

10. Draw the outline of a witch on a piece of wood and burn it before sunrise. This is a common cure for:
    A. purging demons from a sick person's body
    B. removing a curse
    C. keeping the Devil away from your home
    D. expelling a specific witch from a coven

11. Tying a knot in a cow's tail or burying an animal upside down behind a barn is used to:
    A. cure hoof-and-mouth disease
    B. stop milk from curdling
    C. create a good harvest in the coming year
    D. prevent sick animals from reproducing

☆ T H E ☆
DEEP SEA DIVER
Test

1. The limitation of diving with a closed-circuit diving system is:
    A. a depth of 300 feet
    B. a depth of 30 feet maximum
    C. in water with a temperature of at least 68 degrees F.
    D. no limitations if the diver is physically fit

2. "Any object wholly or partly immersed in liquid is buoyed up by a force equal to the weight of the liquid it displaces." This statement is known as:
    A. Cousteau's Rule
    B. Archimedes' Law
    C. The Buoyancy Principle
    D. Hartford's Theory of Compensation

3. "The amount of gas that will dissolve in a liquid at a given temperature is almost directly proportional to the partial pressure of the gas." This statement refers to the dangers of nitrogen narcosis and is known as:
    A. Henry's Law of Gases
    B. Dalton's Theory of Underwater Pressure
    C. the Bend's Theory
    D. decompression and relativity

4. Wet suits are made of:
    A. canvas

    B. neoprene rubber
    C. vinyl
    D. a combination of pure rubber and vinyl

5. A depth gauge determines a diver's depth by:
    A. measuring the amount of air used at that depth
    B. determining the difference between the surface temperature and the depth temperature
    C. measuring the water pressure
    D. comparing the underwater distance from the surface distance

6. It's always a good idea to carry a copy of the decompression table when your dive:
    A. is to any depth
    B. is scheduled for more then 33 feet
    C. is scheduled for more than 90 feet
    D. is scheduled for a depth of 160 feet or more

7. Closed-circuit diving equipment differs from standard diving equipment in that:
    A. The tanks are lighter.
    B. The tanks are heavier.
    C. The tanks contain oxygen.
    D. The tanks contain compressed air.

8. Underwater, water increases one atmosphere, or 14.7 pounds per square inch, every:
    A. 10 feet
    B. 22 feet
    C. 33 feet
    D. 44 feet

9. Fresh water is heavier than salt water and during a freshwater dive, you might have to remove weights from your weight belt.
    True   False

10. The major cause of death during a dive is:

A. hypothermia
B. drowning
C. carbon monoxide poisoning
D. the bends

11. Rapture of the Deep is also known as:
    A. carbon monoxide poisoning
    B. shallow water blackout
    C. salt water sickness
    D. nitrogen narcosis

12. When fully charged, a standard size air tank holds approximately:
    A. 50 cubic feet of air under 3,000 pounds of pressure
    B. 60 cubic feet of air under 1,000 pounds of pressure
    C. 80 cubic feet of air under 3,000 pounds of pressure
    D. 100 cubic feet of air under 5,000 pounds of pressure

13. Holding your breath as you ascend from a deep dive causes the compressed air in your lungs to shrink as the water pressure increases and could result in a ruptured lung.
    True   False

14. Hookah gear is:
    A. designed for use in waters over 500 feet in depth—the air supply is carried in specially-designed underwater tanks strapped to the diver's back
    B. designed for use in shallow waters with the air supply on the surface
    C. used only by military divers
    D. should never be recommended for shallow water dives

15. Underwater, sound travels:
    A. at a slower speed than it does in the air
    B. at the same speed as light
    C. at 4,800 feet per second
    D. at 17,000 feet per second

☆ T H E ☆
CULTURAL LITERACY
——————— *Test* ———————

The National Endowment of the Arts studied the state of arts education in grades kindergarten through 12 and reported that basic arts education is not available in the United States. Most elementary school classroom teachers have had little or no formal training in the arts, and nowhere in the country is there any systematic, comprehensive, and formal assessment of student achievements in the arts. In 1962 and again in 1985, the organization learned that 61 percent of American adults had not attended a live performance of jazz, classical music, musical theater, and ballet in the past twelve months and had not visited an art gallery or museum.

This quiz on cultural literacy was prepared by staff members of the National Endowment of the Arts. Scoring well on the test doesn't mean you are culturally literate but these questions may suggest areas you would like to know more about.

1. The *War of the Worlds* was:
   A. a science fiction novel that spawned the "Flash Gordon" TV series
   B. a radio broadcast that terrified the nation over the fictitious landing of Martians on Earth
   C. an autobiographical account of one soldier's combat life during World War I
   D. a series of stories and poetry about the Crusades.

2. Which of the following design professions shapes our cities and towns and the products we see and use?
   A. architecture
   B. industrial design
   C. fashion design
   D. all of the above

3. The paintings of this deceased American artist included Marilyn Monroe and soup cans.
   A. Andy Warhol
   B. Salvador Dali
   C. Georgia O'Keefe
   D. Jackson Pollock

4. On the following, who has not been poet laureate of the United States?
   A. Robert Frost
   B. Richard Wilbur
   C. Robert Penn Warren
   D. Howard Nemerov

5. Which instrument does not belong?
   A. clarinet
   B. cornet
   C. oboe
   D. bassoon

6. Who wrote the oratorio "Messiah"?
   A. Aaron Copland
   B. W.A. Mozart
   C. Johannes Brahms
   D. G.F. Handel

7. What was the name of Charles Kane's sled in *Citizen Kane*?
   A. Racer
   B. Rosebud
   C. Big Jake
   D. Calamity Jane

8. In which region of the country can totem poles be found?
   A. the desert southwest
   B. Alaska
   C. the northern Rockies
   D. the Great Plains

9. The style of neoimpressionist painter George Seurat is known as:
   A. cubism
   B. romanticism
   C. pointillism
   D. surrealism

10. "Falling Water" is:
    A. a house designed by Frank Lloyd Wright
    B. an Auguste Rodin sculpture
    C. a nineteenth-century ballet
    D. the country's largest statue, dedicated at the base of the U.S. side of Niagara Falls

11. Who were Charlie Parker, John Coltrane, and Charles Mingus?
    A. early movie directors and pioneers of the first talkies
    B. three twentieth-century black writers who wrote inspiring stories of people struggling for freedom and equality
    C. a teen-age trio that incorporated three-part harmony into the American musical tradition
    D. legendary jazz musicians

12. Who does not belong in this group?
    A. George Balanchine
    B. Martha Graham
    C. Irving Berlin
    D. Fred Astaire

13. The three primary colors are:
    A. Red, green, and blue
    B. Green, blue, and yellow

C. Red, white, and blue
D. Blue, red, and yellow

14. Name the city that gave birth to the design of the first skyscraper.
    A. New York
    B. Chicago
    C. Philadelphia
    D. Paris

15. Who wrote *Bonfire of the Vanities*?
    A. William Faulkner
    B. Tom Wolfe
    C. F. Scott Fitzgerald
    D. Ernest Hemingway

16. Who was not part of "the lost generation"?
    A. William Faulkner
    B. Ezra Pound
    C. F. Scott Fitzgerald
    D. Ernest Hemingway

17. Match the author with the work:
    1. *The Adventures of Huckleberry Finn*   A. J.D. Salinger
    2. *1984*   B. Samuel Clemens
    3. *Native Son*   C. William Shakespeare
    4. *Last of the Mohicans*   D. John Keats
    5. *Ode on a Grecian Urn*   E. George Orwell
    6. *The Taming of the Shrew*   F. Richard Wright
    7. *Catcher in the Rye*   G. James F. Cooper

☆ T H E ☆
BARTENDER
Test

1. An extra dry martini is garnished with:
   A. an olive
   B. a lemon twist
   C. a lime wedge
   D. none of the above

2. The proof of a spirit is:
   A. a way of expressing its alcoholic quality
   B. twice the percentage of alcohol by volume
   C. half the percentage of alcohol by volume
   D. a guaranteed standard of quality

3. Which of the following has the highest alcohol content?
   A. 8 ounces of 11% wine
   B. a 12-ounce mug of 5% beer
   C. a highball with 1 ounce of 80-proof gin
   D. a martini with 2 ounces of 80-proof gin and ¼ ounce of 19% vermouth

4. Using the recipe cost method, calculate the selling price of the following recipe based on beverage costs of 18% of total cost of the drink
   Martini—2 ounces of gin at $6.75 per liter
   　　　　　¼ ounce of vermouth at $2.54 per 750 milliliters
   　　　　　2 olives (100 olives at $2.50 per jar)
   A. $2.63

B. $1.53
C. $3.08
D. $3.79

5. The recommended bar stock for a liquor storeroom is:
   A. the maximum stock level
   B. one-and-a-half times the expected consumption for the purchase period
   C. twice the heaviest expected consumption for the purchase period
   D. the reorder point

6. Which of the following is not an accepted method of measuring liquor for drinks?
   A. weighing it
   B. metering the pour
   C. using a lined jigger
   D. free pouring

7. At the end of the evening, leftover cherries, olives, and onions should be discarded.
   True   False

8. A Seven and Seven is made with seven ingredients.
   True   False

9. Which of the following is normally not aged?
   A. gin
   B. bourbon
   C. rye
   D. brandy

10. A successful mixed drink is based on a tested recipe that should include:
    A. the exact amount of each ingredient
    B. the exact brand name of liquor to be used
    C. the glass size
    D. Both A and C are correct.

Using the ingredients as clues, can you identify the following drinks and cocktails?

11. Take the juice of 2 limes, 2 teaspoons of powdered sugar, and 2 ounces of carbonated water. Fill a 12-ounce Tom Collins glass with shaved ice and stir until glass is frosted. Add 2 dashes of bitter and 2½ ounces of rum. Stir and decorate with a slice of lemon, orange, pineapple, and cherry. Serve with straws.

12. Add the juice of half a lemon to 2 ounces of dry gin, ½ ounce wild-cherry-flavored brandy and, 1 teaspoon of powdered sugar. Shake well with cracked ice and strain into a 12-ounce Tom Collins glass. Add ice cubes and fill with carbonated water. Stir and decorate with fruits in season. Serve with straws.

13. Pour 8 ounces of cold beer in a 12-ounce glass and add 4 ounces of cold V8 or tomato juice slowly. Add a dash of salt and a dash of pepper. Stir.

14. Add ¾ ounce of green creme de menthe to ¾ ounce of white creme de cacao and ¾ ounce of light sweet cream. Shake well with cracked ice and strain into 3-ounce cocktail glass.

15. Mix 1 ounce of unsweetened pineapple juice with the juice of 1 lime, the juice of 1 small orange, 1 teaspoon of powdered sugar, ½ ounce of apricot brandy, 2½ ounces of rum, 1 ounce of Jamaican rum, and 1 ounce of passion fruit juice. Add cracked ice and agitate for a full minute in electric mixer or shake in cocktail mixer. Strain into a 14-ounce glass. Decorate with square of pineapple and one green and one red cherry.

☆ THE ☆
CHESS MASTER
——— *Test* ———

1. Based on four moves for white and four moves for black, how many possible positions can arise in the first four moves in a game of chess?
   A. 1,000
   B. 5,000
   C. 10,000
   D. 15,000

2. How many positions can arise in the first ten moves?
   A. 25,000
   B. 169,519,829,100,544,000,000,000,000,000
   C. 75 quintillion

3. The first chess match played by telegraph was in:
   A. 1865
   B. 1844
   C. 1902

4. The first international chess tournament was held in:
   A. 1859
   B. 1575
   C. 1492

5. Tebuchadnezzer, the Greek philosopher Xerxes, and Ulysses have all been credited with having invented the game of chess.
   True   False

6. The popularity of chess throughout the ages can be con-
   firmed by the fact that the second book ever printed in the
   English language was a chess book.
   True   False

7. Had it not been for the game of chess, the American
   Revolution might well have been lost.
   True   False

8. World Champion Bobby Fischer never lost a chess match.
   True   False

9. The longest game ever played in tournament competition
   lasted:
   A. 174 moves
   B. 193 moves
   C. 228 moves

10. The shortest game ever played in tournament competition
    lasted:
    A. one move
    B. two moves
    C. half a move

11. Chess, in one form or another, at one time or another, has
    been banned by the Catholic Church, Islam, and the
    USSR.
    True   False

12. How many people in the United States know how to play
    chess?
    A. 1 million
    B. 15 million
    C. 30 million

13. The Knight's Tour, defined as placing a knight on any
    square and leaping to all the squares on the board without
    touching the same square, can be accomplished in how
    many different ways?

A. 10,000
B. 100,000
C. 31,000,000

14. Who said: "Chess is a foolish expedient for making idle people believe they are doing something very clever when they are only wasting their time."
    A. George Bernard Shaw
    B. T.S. Eliot
    C. H.G. Wells

15. Who said: "Chess is everything—art, science and sport."
    A. Boris Spassky
    B. Robert Fischer
    C. Anatoly Karpov

16. One of the most unusual chess tournaments took place in Prague in 1874. The participants were:
    A. bald
    B. blindfolded
    C. handcuffed

☆ T H E ☆
MISS AMERICA™
CONTESTANT
Test

The Miss America Pageant is held in Atlantic City every year. To enter, contestants must meet certain basic requirements and abide by all the rules of the local, state, and national Miss America Pageants. The following questions are related to contestant requirements in the pageant and knowledge of previous pageants.

1. The national ruling for all of the preliminary pageants is that total time for a contestant in the talent competition is:
   A. 3 minutes and 30 seconds
   B. 1 minute and 45 seconds
   C. 2 minutes and 50 seconds
   D. 4 minutes

2. If you sing, dance, or play an instrument in the talent competition and need accompaniment, you may not use a prerecorded tape.
   True   False

3. The first Miss America Pageant was held in Atlantic City in:
   A. 1921
   B. 1923
   C. 1925
   D. 1927

4. To qualify for entry in the Miss American Pageant, the entrant must be a female between the ages of:
   A. 16 and 28
   B. 17 and 26
   C. 18 and 26
   D. 18 and 28

5. The Miss American Pageant is always held in:
   A. August
   B. September
   C. October
   D. the first Sunday after Labor Day

6. You must be a high school graduate to compete in the Miss America Pageant.
   True   False

7. The winner of the Miss America Pageant receives a scholarship valued at:
   A. $15,000
   B. $20,000
   C. $35,000
   D. $50,000

8. The first Miss America Pageant was held in Atlantic City:
   A. to show the state's appreciation for women's contributions to society
   B. to draw tourists into the area
   C. because New York City turned down the event
   D. because the first scholarship awards were sponsored by a local bank

9. If you've been married and are now single due to a divorce or your husband's death, you cannot compete as a Miss America contestant.
   True   False

10. The last Miss America to be crowned in a swimsuit was Miss America of:
    A. 1943
    B. 1945

C. 1947
D. 1949

11. The first college student to be crowned Miss America was:
    A. Deborah Bryant in 1966
    B. Jean Bartel in 1943
    C. Evelyn Ay in 1954
    D. Sharon Ritchie in 1956

12. The first Miss America Pageant was televised on ABC-TV in 1954. The winner that year was:
    A. Lee Meriwether
    B. Mary Ann Mobley
    C. Linda Mead
    D. Nancy Fleming

13. The first Miss America Pageant was originally called:
    A. The Atlantic City Miss America Beauty Pageant
    B. The Atlantic City Bathing Beauty Contest
    C. The U.,S. Beauty Contest
    D. The American Beauty Rose

14. The first Miss America Achievement Award was awarded to:
    A. Joan Collins
    B. Betty Ford
    C. Bella Abzug
    D. Jackie Onassis

15. A contestant may compete at the state level as many times as she wants, but may only compete in the national competition once.
    True   False

☆ THE ☆
WASHINGTON, D.C., TOUR GUIDE
― Test ―

1. The Smithsonian Institution is located:
    A. between Constitution Avenue and 5th Street
    B. between Arlington Boulevard and North Capitol Street
    C. between 4th and 14th Streets
    D. Massachusetts Avenue and 34th Street

2. The Washington Monument is:
    A. 222 feet high
    B. 333 feet high
    C. 555 feet high
    D. 666 feet high

3. The Iwo Jima statue is based on a photograph by photographer Joe Rosenthal taken on:
    A. August 26, 1942
    B. July 23, 1944
    C. February 23, 1945
    D. December 6, 1943

4. The John F. Kennedy Center for the Performing Arts:
    A. is 630 feet long and 300 feet wide
    B. is faced with marble
    C. contains six different theaters
    D. Both A and B are correct.
    E. Both B and C are correct.

5. In the last 30 years, the Washington Monument has settled:
   A. one inch
   B. two inches
   C. one foot
   D. two feet

6. To get to the top of the Washington Monument, you must ascend by elevator because the steps are closed to climbers. To descend, you have the option of taking the elevator or walking down the:
   A. 684 steps
   B. 782 steps
   C. 898 steps
   D. over 1,000 steps

7. The museum located at 12th Street and Constitution Avenue is the:
   A. National Museum of American History
   B. National Museum of Natural History
   C. National Air and Space Museum
   D. National Museum of Modern Art

8. The structure known as "The Castle" in Washington, D.C., is:
   A. the White House
   B. the Senate Building
   C. the Smithsonian Building
   D. the Old National Building Museum

9. The Vietnam Veterans' Memorial is made up of:
   A. one wall with 58 panels listing 35,000 names
   B. two walls with 140 panels listing almost 60,000 names
   C. four walls with 100 panels listing all of the names of those who served in Vietnam
   D. a series of walls and panels listing 40,000 names in alphabetical order

10. The Washington Cathedral's design is based on:
    A. the fourteenth-century English and French Gothic style
    B. the early Russian Revolution style
    C. a specific cathedral in England that dates back to the twelfth century
    D. The sixteenth-century French Renaissance style

11. On an average day, about _____ persons visit the White House.
    A. 2,500
    B. 4,000
    C. 6,000
    D. over 10,000

Match the A, B, and C answers below with the rooms of the White House listed in Questions 12, 13, and 14.
    A. used for receptions, balls, concerts, weddings, press conferences, and bill-signing ceremonies
    B. used for small teas and receptions
    C. used to receive guests and receptions and state dinners

12. the Green Room
    A._____ B._____ C._____

13. the East Room
    A._____ B._____ C._____

14. the Blue Room
    A._____ B._____ C._____

15. The books in the Library of Congress occupy:
    A. over 25 miles of shelves
    B. over 250 miles of shelves
    C. over 500 miles of shelves
    D. over 1,000 miles of shelves

★ T H E ★
PROFESSIONAL GOLFER
—————— *Test* ——————

The Professional Golfers' Association of America was formed to elevate the standards of the vocation of professional golf and to promote interest in the game of golf. In order to be eligible to apply for membership in the association, an applicant must be a citizen of the United States or a resident alien who has lived in the United States for a minimum of five years, and be over 21 years of age. The applicant must have completed a PGA-approved training course and be registered in the apprentice program at the time of application. Applicants must be the head golf professional at a recognized club or course or be employed as an assistant golf professional to a Class A member. Applicants must pass a standardized written examination and successfully complete an interview administered by the association.

1. What city in Scotland is recognized as the birthplace of golf?
   A. Edinburgh
   B. St. Andrews
   C. Aberdeen
   D. Dundee

2. What organization establishes the rules of golf?
   A. the Professional Golfers' Association
   B. the U.S. Golf Association
   C. the International Golf Society

3. Who has the most lifetime victories on the PGA tour?
   A. Sam Snead
   B. Ben Hogan
   C. Jack Nicklaus
   D. Arnold Palmer

4. What term is used when a golfer scores a three on a par-five hole?
   A. Eagle
   B. Birdie
   C. Ace
   D. Bogie

5. Years ago, golf clubs were referred to by names instead of numbers. What name was given to the present day three-wood?
   A. iron
   B. spoon
   C. stick
   D. randy

6. Who was the first player on the PGA Tour to exceed $1 million in earnings in one year?
   A. Jack Nicklaus
   B. Curtis Strange
   C. Greg Norman
   D. Arnold Palmer

7. On what golf course is the Masters played?
   A. Pebble Beach
   B. Pinehurst
   C. Augusta National

8. Where is the Golf Hall of Fame located?
   A. Pinehurst
   B. St. Andrews, Scotland
   C. Far Hills, New Jersey

9. What is the name of the championship which pits amateur golfers from the United States against Great Britain?

A. The Porter Cup
B. The Walker Cup
C. The Anglo-American Cup

10. What golfer holds the record for the lowest score in a 72-hole PGA event?
A. Doug Ford
B. Mike Souchak
C. Billy Casper

11. What golfer is nicknamed "The Golden Bear?"
A. Sandy Lyle
B. Greg Norman
C. Jack Nicklaus

12. The first player to shoot 59 in a PGA tournament was:
A. Ben Hogan
B. Al Gerberger
C. Lee Trevino

13. In 1989, Curtis Strange became the first golfer in more than 30 years to win back-to-back U.S. Open titles. On what course did he win his second championship?
A. Oak Hill
B. Oak Tree
C. Oakmont

14. The maximum number of golf clubs allowed by the rules is:
A. 12
B. 14
C. 16

15. The old name for the five-iron was:
A. the niblock
B. the mashie
C. the cleek

☆ T H E ☆
BOMB DISPOSAL
—————— *Test* ——————

Bomb disposal experts in the Army, Navy, Marines, and Air Force are called "Explosive Ordnance Disposal Technicians" and are responsible for emergencies involving explosive items both military and civilian. This includes the identification, neutralization, and disposal of unexploded military ordnance like bombs, artillery shells, mortars, etc. They're called upon to assist civilian officials in dealing with bomb threats and the disposal of explosives like dynamite and hazardous devices. In addition to explosive ordnance, EOD personnel also deal with chemical and biological substances and incidents involving nuclear weapons.

EOD personnel stationed in Europe and Asia are often called upon to dispose of items dating back to early wars, so an understanding of all types of ordnance—regardless of age—is required. EOD personnel stationed in the Washington, D.C., and Virginia area regularly deal with ordnance dating back to the Civil War.

The following questions are similar to the questions used on Explosive Ordnance Disposal qualification examinations.

1. You're called upon to remove a 500-pound U.S. high-explosive bomb discovered at a site that was once an active Air Force practice bombing range. Upon examination, you discover only a portion of the side of the bomb is sticking out of the ground. The nose and tail section of

the bomb are completely buried. Appraising the situation, you would assume:
A. There's a fuse located in the nose only.
B. There's a fuse located in the tail only.
C. There's a fuse located in the nose and the tail.
D. There are no fuses in the bomb because fuses were never used on bombs dropped on practice bombing ranges.

2. Before moving a hand grenade that has misfired to a location where it can be disposed of safely, you should:
A. Locate the handle, push it into position, and replace the firing pin.
B. Jar it remotely.
C. Fire a bullet into it from a safe distance.
D. Remove the explosive content through the filler hole in the bottom.

3. TNT can be safely burned.
A. True
B. False

4. One means of identifying bombs dating back to World War II is by tail-fin configuration. Different countries used different configurations. British bombs used during that period usually had tail fins that were:
A. square
B. triangular
C. round
D. octagonal

5. American bombs had tail fins that were:
A. square
B. triangular
C. round
D. octagonal

6. Depth charges are usually activated by:
A. contact with a submarine or the ocean bottom

    B. impact with the water
    C. a change in water pressure
    D. the magnetic influence of a submarine or ship's keel

7. Moored sea mines are usually anchored by:
    A. a chain attached to the bottom
    B. a heavy weight floating at the end of a steel cable
    C. a flotation ring
    D. a ship's anchor

8. Long-delay bomb fuses used by the U.S. during World War II had delays ranging from minutes to hours. These delays were accomplished:
    A. using a clockwork device
    B. using a chemical action
    C. using a combination clockwork-chemical action
    D. using electronic circuitry with impregnated chips
    E. using slow-burning pyrotechnic fuses ignited when the bomb was dropped from the aircraft

9. Long-delay bomb fuses used by the U.S. during World War II were usually located:
    A. in the tail
    B. in the nose
    C. in the tail and nose
    D. in the side of the bomb, hidden from view by a sheet metal plate riveted over the fuse cavity

10. What wind velocity would be cause to cancel an open burning operation on the disposal range?
    A. 4 miles per hour
    B. 8 mile per hour
    C. 12 miles per hour
    D. 16 miles per hour

11. A mortar shell is usually armed and considered capable of exploding:
    A. immediately after it leaves the barrel
    B. just prior to impact with the ground

C. at the end of its arc after reaching maximum altitude
D. when it reaches its maximum speed and trajectory after firing

12. A plastic covered safety fuse burns at a rate of:
    A. 30 seconds per foot
    B. 40 seconds per foot
    C. 30-45 seconds per foot
    D. 30-40 seconds per foot

13. A galvanometer is used to:
    A. check the continuity of wiring for an electrical detonation
    B. testing the amount of explosives required to detonate a steel girder
    C. measuring the amount of wire needed to set off a remote explosive with a blasting box
    D. test the batteries in a flashlight

14. You're called to investigate a suspicious-looking package located near a mailbox on a street corner. The package is wrapped in brown paper and tied with string. The first thing you should do is:
    A. probe the package with a steel rod to determine the contents
    B. evacuate the area
    C. cut the string and remove the paper
    D. attach a small charge to it and blow it up

15. One of the characteristics of C-4 explosive is that it:
    A. is pliable
    B. is solid like dynamite
    C. will detonate by firing a rifle bullet into it
    D. can be used to fill blasting caps in the field

16. Military bomb disposal personnel in England were once know as:
    A. ordinance doctors
    B. sappers
    C. firemen
    D. sure-firers

☆ T H E ☆
CHINESE COOK
Test

1. Chinese food has often been compared to:
   A. Japanese food
   B. the French art culinaire
   C. southern American food
   D. Mexican food

2. A popular substitute for milk in Chinese cooking is:
   A. yogurt
   B. bean curd
   C. vanilla flavoring
   D. cream cheese

3. Two of the most popular dishes served in restaurants in China are sweet-and-sour pork and Egg Foo Young.
   True   False

4. The main ingredients in sweet-and-sour sauce are:
   A. sugar, vinegar, and mixed fruits
   B. sugar, food coloring
   C. cream and pineapples
   D. soy sauce and cream

5. Shao hsing is also called Chinese:
   A. meat and potatoes
   B. yellow rice
   C. almond cake
   D. noodle soup

6. The Chinese food served in the United States is very different from the Chinese food served in China.
   True   False

7. The difference between regional cuisines like Cantonese, Szechwan, Hunan, and Peking are mainly due to the local produce used, the spices, and the cooking style.
   True   False

8. Chinese birds' nest soup is made from:
   A. discarded robin eggs
   B. the twigs and vegetation found in birds' nests
   C. the saliva of cave-dwelling swifts
   D. the discarded eggs of any small bird

9. MSG, or monosodium glutamate, is added to Chinese food:
   A. as a preservative
   B. as a flavoring
   C. to add color
   D. all of the above

10. During an authentic Chinese banquet, often two soups are served to:
    A. wash down the entrées
    B. offer a contrast in taste—one sweet, the other often sour
    C. insures the diners don't go away from the table hungry
    D. clear the palate

11. At most authentic Chinese banquets, an even number of courses are generally served.
    True   False

12. A wok must be used to cook authentic Chinese food.
    True   False

13. When cooking Chinese food on an electric range, it is

better to use a regular pan instead of a wok because the heat will be more evenly distributed.
True   False

14. Generally speaking, Cantonese cuisine is mild, delicate, and sort of bland.
True   False

15. Grilling, pan frying, and baking are traditional methods of authentic Chinese cooking.
True   False

16. Boiling and simmering are not traditional methods of Chinese cooking.
True   False

17. Fish is a symbol of plenty in China and it is the traditional Chinese custom that all guests:
    A. eat all of the fish as a symbol of plenty and prosperity
    B. leave a small portion of each dish served with the fish as a symbol of prosperity
    C. leave the last bite of fish as a symbol they will not run out of food
    D. pass a portion of fish to the guest on their right

18. The color of soy sauce comes from its natural ingredients.
True   False

19. The fortune cookie was invented by a Chinese monk.
True   False

20. In the Orient, Chinese restaurants serve spring rolls instead of egg rolls.
True   False

21. Dim-Sum is an authentic Cantonese dish which translated means hardy Oriental hors d'oeuvres served with tea.
True   False

☆ T H E ☆
LONDON TAXI DRIVER
Test

There are an estimated 19,500 taxi drivers in London and each has passed what is considered to be the most stringent taxi driver test in the world. Starting wages average about $15 an hour and beginning drivers pay a fee to the taxi-leasing company of about $240 a week plus the cost of gasoline. A London taxi driver test consists of thousands of questions relating to the shortest distance between two points in the city and the driver's knowledge of London. The Metropolitan School of Knowledge in London, the leading taxi driver training facilities, estimates the average driver spends three years in training before he is qualified to take the test. In addition to routing questions, the London taxi drivers are expected to have a general knowledge of London's history, attractions, hotels, and information of interest to visitors. The following questions are similar to those on the London Taxi Driver Test:

1. The United States Embassy is located at:
   A. No. 1 Grosvenor Square
   B. 64 Trafalgar Square
   C. at the north end of Haymarket
   D. opposite Victoria Station

2. The speed limit in downtown London is:
   A. 25 miles per hour
   B. 30 miles per hour

C. 40 miles per hour
D. 45 miles per hour

3. The top speed allowed on the major motorways is:
   A. 70 miles per hour
   B. 80 miles per hour
   C. 90 miles per hour
   D. There is no speed limit on the major motorways. You drive at a speed that is considered safe for conditions.

4. The British Imperial gallon is larger than the American gallon.
   True   False

5. The cost of taking a taxi from Heathrow Airport to Piccadilly Circus in downtown London is approximately:
   A. 4 pounds
   B. 8 pounds
   C. 12 pounds
   D. 15 pounds

6. The Intercontinental Hotel is located:
   A. on Kensington High Street
   B. on Hyde Park Corner
   C. at Knightsbridge
   D. at Hamilton Place

7. Fulham Road is well-known for:
   A. night life
   B. antique shops and boutiques
   C. a weekend farmer's market
   D. embassy row

8. Westminster Abbey is located on:
   A. Marylebone Road
   B. Parliament Square
   C. Regent's Park Road
   D. Tower Hill

9. The Old Vic is located on:
   A. St. Martin's Lane
   B. Hungerford Arches
   C. Waterloo Road
   D. Shaftesbury Avenue

10. You may add an additional ten pence per mile to your standard mileage fare:
    A. between 8 PM and 6 AM
    B. after midnight until 6 AM
    C. only when traveling outside the immediate downtown area
    D. for each passenger over one

11. Visitors to London might be interested in special passes that allow travel on all London Transport buses for an inclusive fee during the summer months. These passes are called:
    A. Red Rovers
    B. London Value Passes
    C. Blue Lines
    D. Transport Tickets

12. The Tower of London is open daily from March to September from:
    A. 8 AM until 8 PM
    B. 9:30 until 9 PM
    C. 9:30 AM until 5 PM
    D. 8 AM until dusk

13. The Bank of London is often referred to as:
    A. The Round House
    B. The Old Lady of Threadneedle Street
    C. The Vault
    D. The Tower Bank of King Street

☆ T H E ☆
KNOW-IT-ALL
—————— Test ——————

1. Which of the following cities have the five busiest airports?
   A. Boston, New York, San Francisco, Los Angeles, and St. Louis
   B. Chicago, Atlanta, Los Angeles, Dallas, and Denver
   C. Chicago, New York, Los Angeles, Miami, and Boston
   D. Boston, New York, Miami, Denver, and Washington D.C.

2. What is the singular of "spaghetti?"
   A. Spaghettia
   B. Spaghetti
   C. Spaghetto
   D. Spaghoti

3. What is the difference between the United Kingdom and Great Britain?
   A. Great Britain is an island made up of England, Scotland, and Wales. The United Kingdom is Great Britain plus Northern Ireland.
   B. Great Britain is an island made up of England, Scotland, Wales, and all of Ireland. The United Kingdom does not recognize any part of Ireland.
   C. Great Britain is an independent island nation and is not connected politically with Scotland and Wales. The United Kingdom is not connected politically with Wales but it does recognize Scotland.

    D. Great Britain claims that northern Ireland is under its
rule. The United Kingdom does not.

4. What percentage of American households have cable TV?
   A. about 50 percent
   B. about 75 percent
   C. about 85 percent
   D. about 90 percent

5. Which of the following flags have one or more stars?
   A. Argentina, Czechoslovakia, Costa Rica, and France
   B. Finland, Israel, South Korea, and Japan
   C. North Korea, Panama, Turkey, and Vietnam
   D. The United States, Haiti, Guatemala, and West Germany

6. When you return from a vacation or trip, you often bring
   back a memento or _____. Do you spell
   that:
   A. souvenier
   B. souvenir
   C. sovenier
   D. souveneer

7. In addition to being movie actors, what do Robert De
   Niro, Erik Estrada, Douglas Fairbanks, Jr., George Burns,
   and Woody Allen have in common?

8. In addition to being movie actors and actresses, what do
   Loni Anderson, Gary Busey, Stockard Channing, Danny
   DeVito, and Michael Douglas have in common?

9. As a well-traveled Know-It-All and Person of the World,
   how high do you think the tallest building in Miami,
   Florida is?
   A. well over 1,000 feet
   B. about 750 feet
   C. about 650 feet
   D. about 550 feet

10. The word "eclipse" comes from the Greek word for:
   A. failing to appear
   B. hidden behind
   C. not visible
   D. only half visible

11. From baseline to baseline, a tennis court is:
   A. 58 feet long
   B. 68 feet long
   C. 78 feet long
   D. 88 feet long

Match the model numbers in Column A with the automobile manufacturers listed in the Column B.

12.	240GL	A.	Lincoln
13.	944S	B.	Honda
14.	J2000	C.	Peugeot
15.	505	D.	Pontiac
16.	RX7	E.	Audi
17.	Mark VII	F.	BMW
18.	CRX	G.	Mercedes
19.	LTD	H.	Ford
20.	280Z	I.	Porsche
21.	4000S	J.	Mazda
22.	535Sis	K.	Datsun
23.	380SEL	L.	Volvo

24. The two most widely used IQ tests are the Terman and Wechsler Tests. Although they differ slightly, these tests rate a genius:
   A. from a low of 111 to a high of 128 or over
   B. from a low of 128 to a high of over 140
   C. from a low of 143 to a high of 180
   D. from a low of 140 to a high of over 200

25. Raw and general intelligence is rated on an IQ scale. According to studies, 50 percent of the United States population has an IQ of:

A. 120-127
B. 91-110
C. 80-86
D. 111-119

26. The solid-colored balls on a pool table are:
    A. numbered with even numbers only
    B. numbered with odd numbers only
    C. numbered from 8 to 15
    D. numbered from 1 to 8

27. The game of quoits is similar to:
    A. volleyball
    B. squash
    C. pocket billiards
    D. horseshoe pitching

28. Although it's not exact science, most experts agree that if
    your son is three feet tall at the age of two years and five
    weeks and your daughter is two feet, eight inches tall
    when she's 13 weeks away from her second birthday,
    there is overwhelming evidence that:
    A. they will both be the same height when they reach the
       age of 16
    B. they will both be well below the average height for
       their age when they're 16
    C. they will both be twice that height when they're adults
    D. they will both be over six feet tall when they're adults

29. You'll burn up more calories swimming or rowing than
    you will pedaling a bicycle at 13 miles an hour.
    True   False

30. All of the skin on your body weighs about:
    A. half of your body weight
    B. a third of your body weight
    C. a quarter of your body weight
    D. a sixth of your body weight

☆ T H E ☆
PRISON GUARD
Test

The New York State Department of Correctional Services administers qualification tests for jail and prison guards and Correction Office positions with assignments at state correction and lockup facilities. Duties include the responsibility for the custody, security, safety, and well-being of criminal offenders. The examination is administered twice a year and at the time of appointment, applicants must be at least 21 years of age with a high school diploma or equivalency. The test consists of a written test, a background investigation and a physical/medical examination. If the written test is passed, applicants are required to participate in a psychological screening process and attend a resident training program before being assigned to a correction or lockup facility.

1. People commit crimes because:
    A. They are mentally ill.
    B. They come from poor families.
    C. It is their way of trying to solve a problem.
    D. They want to.
    E. They are born criminals.

2. The best procedure to follow when a prisoner is upset from a visit from his wife or girl friend is to:
    A. lock him in his cell by himself so he will not try to escape and where he will not disturb others

B. permit him to call his wife or girl friend and correct the misunderstanding
C. talk to the prisoner or at least be a sympathetic and understanding listener
D. refuse to let further visits take place if he is continuously having problems because of arguments with his visitors

3. In which of the following situations is handcuffing or other physical restraint *most* likely to be needed?
    A. An inmate seems to have lost control of his senses and is banging his fists repeatedly against the bars of his cell.
    B. During the past two weeks, an inmate has deliberately tried to start three fights with other inmates.
    C. An inmate claims to be sick and refuses to leave his cell for a scheduled meal.
    D. During the night, an inmate begins to shout and sing, disturbing the sleep of others.

4. As a guard, you've been assigned to duty at a vehicle entrance point in the prison. Which of the following is probably the *best* method of preventing the movement of unauthorized persons in vehicles?
    A. If passenger identifications are checked when vehicle enters, no check is necessary when the vehicle leaves.
    B. Passenger identification should be checked for all vehicles when vehicle enters and when it leaves.
    C. Passenger identification need not be checked when a vehicle enters but should always be checked when a vehicle leaves.
    D. Except for official vehicles, passenger identification should be checked when vehicle enters and when it leaves.

5. One of the guards in the lockup is a large man and very sure of himself. When a prisoner refused to come out of his cell to take a shower, the guard went in and took him out. Do you think this was the proper thing to do?
    A. Yes. Prisoners should do what they're told.

B. No. The prisoner should have been permitted to remain in the cell until he decided to come out.

C. Yes. Prisoners must conform to all schedules.

D. No. The officer should have not gone in the cell alone.

6. Indicate whether the following statements are true or false:
   A. Homosexuals can be easily identified.
      True   False
   B. A person who talks to himself is psychotic.
      True   False
   C. People who threaten suicide will not attempt it.
      True   False
   D. People who threaten suicide are just trying to get sympathy.
      True   False
   E. Young people have a high suicide rate.
      True   False
   F. The best method of handling a person who is threatening suicide is to call his bluff.
      True   False
   G. Keeping suicide risks isolated from others is the best way to manage them.
      True   False

7. Prisoner Y is slim and has a limp-wristed feminine appearance. Prisoner W is husky and aggressive. Prisoner Y pretty much minds his own business and does his time. Prisoner W is loud and is trying very hard to become friends with Prisoner Y. He keeps offering Prisoner Y cigarettes and candy which Prisoner Y refuses. What do you suspect is happening?
   A. Nothing. Prisoner W is just trying to be friendly.
   B. Obviously Prisoner Y is a homosexual and Prisoner W doesn't realize it.
   C. Prisoner Y may or may not be a homosexual. His behavior so far does not indicate that he is. Prisoner W, however, is acting like an aggressive homosexual and trying to get closer to Prisoner Y.
   D. none of the above

8. A prisoner is brought to jail with the following symptoms: shakiness, staggering, thick speech, and a blank, glassy-eyed look. The *best* action to take is:
   A. to assume he's drunk and place him in the drunk tank.
   B. figure he might be drunk, but refer him to a doctor because he may also have a serious injury or illness
   C. both of the above
   D. none of the above

9. In making a routine search of an inmate's cell, a guard finds various items. Although there is no immediate danger, he is not sure whether the inmate is permitted to have one of these items. Of the following, the *best* action for the office to take is to:
   A. confiscate the item immediately
   B. give the inmate the benefit of the doubt and let him keep the item
   C. consult his rule book or his supervising officer to find out whether the inmate is permitted to have the item
   D. leave the item in the inmate's cell, but plan to report him for an infraction of the rules

10. A prisoner becomes abusive toward another prisoner and they are on the edge of fighting when a guard arrives on the scene. Both prisoners continue to argue and a shoving contest begins. The guard should:
    A. step between the prisoners and separate them
    B. grab one of the prisoners and pull him away
    C. shout to both prisoners to stop
    D. call another guard for assistance and then step in

☆ T H E ☆
FRENCH INTERPRETER
Test

Translate the phrases and words listed below by choosing the correct answer in English:

1. Mettez mes bagages dans le taxi.
   A. I think I left my bags in the taxi.
   B. Put my luggage into the taxi.
   C. Tell the taxi driver to unload the bags.
   D. Take my bags and call me a taxi.

2. Je ne prendrai pas l'auto hors du pays.
   A. I will not take the car out of the country.
   B. I don't have a car so we can't take a drive in the country.
   C. The car is all paid for.
   D. I don't have permission to drive the car.

3. Y a-t-il une pharmacie près d'ici?
   A. How many miles down the road is the doctor's office?
   B. Can I have a prescription filled here?
   C. Is there a drugstore near here?
   D. Why do you have to go to the pharmacy?

4. L'essence est-elle chère dans ce pays?
   A. Is that a gas station over there?
   B. Is gasoline expensive in this country?
   C. Can I get some gasoline from that pump over there?
   D. Where is the gasoline station?

5. Cette nappe n'est pas propre.
   A. This napkin is wrinkled.
   B. This tablecloth isn't clean.
   C. I want to take a nap.
   D. This is the linen for the bed.

6. Il voudrait de la glace.
   A. He would like some ice cream.
   B. She would like to replace the window.
   C. He would like to go ice skating.
   D. She would like to throw a snowball.

7. Il y a une erreur dans l'addition.
   A. There's something wrong with the arithmetic course.
   B. He can't subtract or add.
   C. There's a bad room in the left wing of the house.
   D. There's a mistake in the bill.

8. Quand part le prochain train?
   A. Is that the last train to the town of Quand?
   B. What time does the next train leave?
   C. Where is the train station?
   D. What do you call that part of the train?

9. Depuis quand êtes-vous malade?
   A. How long have you eaten marmalade on your biscuits?
   B. How long have you been sick?
   C. Is this the fourth time you've been sick?
   D. Do you get seasick on a boat?

10. Combien de temps dois-je attendre?
    A. Is that a long building?
    B. How long is that building?
    C. How long must I wait?
    D. Is there a waiting room around here?

11. Après-demain
    A. the day after tomorrow
    B. yesterday

C. tomorrow
D. later tonight

12. Quand est-ce que nous nous rencontrerons?
    A. Can you make it four days from now?
    B. When does the last trolley car run?
    C. When shall we meet?
    D. Is there room for your family?

13. Je n'ai rien à declarer.
    A. I have nothing to declare.
    B. I have something to declare.
    C. Well, I do declare.
    D. I'll declare it later at the border.

14. Ce chemin est glissant lorsqu'il est mouille.
    A. The house is located on a hill
    B. The road is winding and long
    C. The road is slippery when wet
    D. The clothes are wrinkled beyond repair

15. Je voudrais manger près de la piscine.
    A. I would like to eat by the swimming pool.
    B. I'm not ready to eat yet.
    C. I think I want something to eat.
    D. I would like to take a drive before dinner.

☆ T H E ☆
GRANDSTAND™
CONTESTANT
— Test —

"Grandstand" is a nationally syndicated quiz show designed to challenge sports fans. The show consists of three games: the Face Off, in which each contestant answers questions about a celebrity teammate; the Fast Break, in which contestants answer questions against the clock; and the Touchdown Round for the finalists.

The following are sports trivia questions similar to those asked on the "Grandstand" show.

1. What hockey Hall of Famer holds the record for most times on a Stanley Cup winner—11?

   _____

2. What is the oldest stadium in the NFL?

   _____

3. What boxing weight class precedes the heavyweight division?

   _____

4. What receiver grabbed Roger Staubach's "Hail Mary" pass in the Cowboys-Vikings 1975 playoff game?

   _____

5. The 1952 Cleveland Indians had three 21-game winners. Name two of them.

6. What American League Team was nicknamed "Harvey's Wallbangers" in 1982?

7. Bob Cousy resigned as the coach of what NBA team in the 1973-1974 season?

8. Who portrayed the title character in the film, "Knute Rockne—All American?"

9. Who, at the age of 35, became the youngest player ever to be inducted into the Baseball Hall of Fame?

10. Who quarterbacked the Cowboys in Super Bowl V?

11. Who did Sugar Ray Leonard defeat to win his first welterweight championship?

12. What university put together nine straight NCAA wrestling championships in the 1970s and 1980s?

13. Mickey Mantle's 565-foot homer off Chuck Stobbs was hit out of what park?

14. Who became the first American to jump from high school directly into the NHL?

15. Who was the first heavyweight boxing champion?

16. Chris Evert is married to what former U.S. Olympic ski team member?

17. What defensive unit was known as the "Killer Bees" in the 1984-1985 NFL season?

18. What golfer won the British Open in 1975, 1977, 1980, 1982, and 1983?

19. Nat Fleisher is the founder of what sports publication?

20. What female tennis player was admonished for disrobing at Wimbledon center court?

21. What former Celtic player played on the 1968 Olympic hoop team?

22. What heavyweight boxing champion started his career as an 18-year-old named Kid Blackie?

23. What university did Willie Gault attend?

24. What pitcher for the Giants was labeled "The Meal Ticket" by his teammates?

25. What was the name of the craft that Dennis Conner captained to the 1987 America's Cup?

☆ T H E ☆
SEXOLOGIST
Test

Frequency of intercourse varies with the ages of the couples. Based on monthly frequencies, match the age groups in Column A with the frequencies listed in Column B.

A		B
1. 18-24	A.	less than 8 times
2. 25-34	B.	about 12 times
3. 35-44	C.	8-11 times
4. 55 and older	D.	about 4 times

5. About seven out of ten American couples practice birth control. The most popular method is:
A. rhythm
B. the pill
C. sterilization
D. IUD

6. The percentage of men who remain virgins during their lifetime is approximately:
A. 2 percent
B. 10 percent
C. 15 percent
D. more than 15 percent

7. What percentage of teenagers who are sexually active report they do not use any form of contraception?

A. about 25 percent
B. slightly more than 50 percent
C. about 65 percent
D. slightly more than 75 percent

8. When men and women divorce, the chances of the men remarrying are greater than the chances of the women remarrying.
   True   False

9. Based on the national average for all age groups, most married couples have intercourse:
   A. less than once a month
   B. two to four times a month
   C. two to three times a week
   D. four or five times a week

10. The reason most single men give for not having intercourse is they were worried about their partner getting pregnant. The reason most single women give is:
    A. They didn't love their partner.
    B. They were afraid of getting pregnant.
    C. It was against their religious beliefs.
    D. It would worsen their relationship.

11. Of women under the age of 50 who have been married one year, what percentage have never experienced an orgasm?
    A. 25 percent
    B. 30 percent
    C. 35 percent
    D. 40 percent

12. Based on national averages and age groups, you're more likely to be married if you're between the ages of:
    A. 30-34
    B. 35-45
    C. 55-64
    D. over 65

13. College-educated men are usually more sexually experienced than men with a high school education only.
True   False

14. In a recent survey, _____ percent of married men polled said they cheat on their wives on a regular basis.
    A. 50 percent
    B. 25 percent
    C. 12 percent
    D. 6 percent

15. The majority of men having extra-marital affairs say:
    A. It was a planned seduction.
    B. It was a spontaneous happening.
    C. It happened when they were out of town on business or vacation.
    D. It happened because they thought they'd fallen in love.

16. The majority of women having extra-marital affairs say:
    A. It was a planned seduction.
    B. It was a spontaneous happening.
    C. It happened when they were out of town on business or vacation.
    D. It happened because they thought they'd fallen in love.

17. The average homosexual male says he engages in sex:
    A. about twice a month
    B. about four times a month
    C. about seven times a month
    D. about ten times a month

☆ T H E ☆
CHARTER BOAT
CAPTAIN
Test

1. You're underway and in doubt about an approaching vessel's intentions. You should sound on the whistle:
   A. one short blast
   B. two short blasts
   C. three short blasts
   D. four or more short blasts
   E. two short blasts and two long blasts

2. You're cruising at night and make out the outline of a dredge working in the channel ahead. Two sets of red lights are visible. Between these sets of lights, you would expect to find:
   A. an opening to the pipeline
   B. a tender servicing the dredge
   C. a barge at anchor
   D. an anchorage

3. While proceeding upstream, you encounter a large vessel. Upon seeing you, the vessel's pilot sounds a long blast of his whistle lasting from eight to ten seconds. This indicates:
   A. The vessel is docking.
   B. The vessel is moving from her berth.
   C. The vessel is aground and needs help.
   D. The way is clear for you to pass.

4. Two vessels are approaching each other head-on. According to the rules of the road, each vessel shall:

A. sound one blast and alter course to starboard
B. sound one blast and alter course to port
C. sound two blasts and alter course to starboard
D. sound two blasts and go full astern

5. You approach another vessel and spot a person standing on the forward deck, slowly raising and lowering his outstretched arms from his sides. This indicates you should:
   A. stay clear since the vessel is aground and you're likely to run aground if you approach any closer
   B. provide assistance because the vessel is in distress
   C. stay clear since the vessel is involved in fishing and you could snag lines or a net
   D. give him a wide berth because he's doing on-board calisthenics

6. Two vessels are running in the same direction, slightly off parallel but obviously on a collision course. One vessel sounds one blast of the whistle. This means:
   A. I intend to hold course and speed.
   B. I will avoid crossing in front of you.
   C. I intend to alter my course to the right.
   D. I do not understand your intentions and I'm awaiting your signal.

7. A vessel displaying two white lights in a vertical line from the forward mast is indicating:
   A. The vessel is in distress.
   B. The vessel is not under command.
   C. The vessel is anchored.
   D. The vessel is towing another vessel.

8. A motorboat is underway at a speed of five knots and is being overtaken by a sailing vessel moving at seven knots. According to the rules of the road:
   A. The motorboat must keep out of the way of the sailboat.
   B. The sailboat must keep out of the way of the motorboat.

C. The motorboat should alter course and speed.

D. The motorboat should stop until the sailboat passes and the way is clear.

9. Three short blasts of the whistle means:
    A. The vessel is altering course to port.
    B. The vessel is altering course to starboard.
    C. The vessel's engines are going astern.
    D. The vessel's captain does not understand your intentions.

10. The fog signal for a motorboat underway at sea is:
    A. firing a gun at one minute intervals
    B. ringing the bell for five seconds every minute
    C. sounding at least one prolonged blast every two minutes
    D. sounding three short blasts in succession

11. You're underway at night and see a green light ahead. This is most probably:
    A. a motorboat, so maintain course and speed
    B. a vessel at anchor, so keep out of the way
    C. a sailing vessel, so keep out of the way
    D. a fishing vessel, so keep out of the way

12. In restricted visibility, a motorboat would blow one prolonged fog signal blast followed by two short blasts when:
    A. It is anchored.
    B. It is aground.
    C. It is altering course.
    D. It is towing another vessel.

13. You're underway at night and see three lights ahead—two white lights in a line with a red light in the middle. You should:
    A. alter your course to the right to avoid a collision
    B. put your engines full astern
    C. maintain course and speed because the other vessel will pass clear
    D. take prompt action to avoid a collision

☆ T H E ☆
BORING PERSON
Test

When asked about boring people, Alan Caruba, founder of The Boring Institute, says it's probably genetic and that boring people are born into families with a long history of producing boring aunts, uncles, cousins, siblings, etc. Sometimes the boring gene skips a generation but boring people will always be surrounded by other boring people. The most common trait of boring people is their need to share every little detail of their life and every thought in their head. The most interesting people are those who remain somewhat of a mystery. Boring people are usually serious, perhaps too serious, and should develop a passion for life and bring enthusiasm to their work and play. There are few insults more devastating than to be called boring. To find out if you're a boring person, answer the questions on this Am I A Boring Person test:

1. People have always found me interesting. They listen to my opinions, anecdotes, and stories at length.
   True   False

2. I have a variety of interests and hobbies but often do not have the time to pursue them all.
   True   False

3. I do watch television a lot, but it's a good mix of shows ranging from Public Television to sporting events.
   True   False

4. I simply do not pay attention to what the younger or older generation is into. It doesn't interest me in the least.
   True   False

5. I can't remember the last time I read a book I really liked.
   True   False

6. I see a lot of movies but they just don't make them like they used to.
   True   False

7. I like people but enjoy the people on television more.
   True   False

8. I've been single or married a long time and think it's the perfect lifestyle.
   True   False

9. Today's comedians are often too raunchy, too disrespectful, and just not that funny.
   True   False

10. I have a wide circle of friends with whom I keep in touch on a regular basis.
    True   False

11. I tend to forget birthdays and anniversaries but then so do most people.
    True   False

12. I'm a take-charge kind of person and people like that about me.
    True   False

13. If not a leader, I'm a good steady worker and respected for this quality.
    True   False

14. I know I'm overweight but I am not really concerned. I expect people to accept me as I am.
    True   False

☆ T H E ☆
PSYCHIC
—————— *Test* ——————

The Association of Psychics offers a degree in Scientific Psychic Parapsychology. The qualification test is based on information contained in the association's training manual, "The Scientific Secrets of How To Be A Psychic and Lay Psychologist" by Harold Cunningham. The association believes that psychic phenomena are explainable and that anyone can be a practicing psychic and lay psychologist by using normal common sense and skills developed to handle client relationships. A passing grade of 80 percent is required to qualify for a certificate. The following questions come directly from the psychic's training manual. Some questions can be answered with one or more answers and are indicated on the test by a (1)—select one answer or (2)—select two answers.

1. Why call yourself a "psychic?" (2)
   A. Because I have as much knowledge and ability as anyone, including other psychics.
   B. Because psychics have mystical powers.
   C. Because many people believe in psychics and I can be more helpful and effective when they believe I have unseen knowledge.

2. What are the main points you must remember in your career as a psychic? (2)

    A. A psychic can give the client hope and easy answers to his problems.

    B. Helping other people, plus exercise, reduces stress and gives one time to solve problems.

    C. Do good, feel good is the way to happiness.

3. When your client seems to be suffering from a dangerous phobia, deep depression, or extreme anger, what should you do first? (1)

    A. Help the client to a hospital or @ed help immediately.

    B. Try to find the root of their problem, then help them find the best treatment.

    C. Question them about their ideas for possible solutions. When they hit on the solution, all you say is, "Are you going to try it?"

4. Your client has a problem and the solution is obvious to you. How do you tell them? (1)

    A. Be blunt and explain the solution.

    B. Realize that they probably know the solution but are not ready to accept it, but you tell them anyway.

    C. Question them about their ideas for possible solutions. When they hit on the right solution all you ask is, "Are you going to try it?"

5. What exactly is a "cold reading?" (2)

    A. a way to convince the client that the psychic knows all about his future

    B. a way to show the client that a psychic does understand him but with expressed honesty about limitations

    C. a way to observe the client's responses so that the psychic can gain more information

6. Your clients are actually searching for answers outside themselves. How do you answer their questions? (1)

    A. Tell them they are just looking for excuses.

    B. Tell them they are trying to blame someone else for their problems.

    C. This is a very complex world. No matter how hard you try you'll never master it. Learn to enjoy the adventure.

7. What are you really doing when you are simply listening? (1)
   A. waiting to respond when they ask a question
   B. teaching
   C. sharing life's problems and waiting for the client to look inside his or herself

8. How long must I listen before I express my opinion during a series of sessions? (1)
   A. 10 weeks
   B. 10 days
   C. You never express an opinion.

9. A client is obviously a hypochondriac, always complaining about his pains and illnesses and how all the doctors have been wrong. How do you answer his questions? (1)
   A. Do what many doctors do, tell him it's all in his mind.
   B. Send him to a psychiatrist.
   C. Tell a story of about how doing things for people and exercising will increase the healing chemicals in a person's body and heal a person when drugs some-time fail. Explain that this should be discussed with the client's doctor.

10. How do you handle a problem when the client thinks that his plans are always stopped if the devil is working against him? (1)
    A. Tell him he expects too much.
    B. Tell a story of how nature is indifferent to our desires and that life is tough. Explain that happiness is often achieved by overcoming the hardships of life.
    C. Agree with your client.

11. Which of these actions is important for the psychic after a reading? (1)
    A. watch the client while talking about an experience with your friends
    B. tell a joke
    C. listen to the client patiently

☆ THE ☆
LUMBERJACK
Test

1. When scalping with a brush cutter blade, the blade should be held approximately:
   A. 5 inches off the ground
   B. directly on the ground
   C. as far above the ground as possible
   D. at a 45-degree angle

2. Kickback on a chain saw occurs when:
   A. The chain reverses direction and creates torque.
   B. The chain stops rotating and jams.
   C. The chain contacts an object at the tip of the guide bar.
   D. The guide bar jams between the cut.

3. Red, silver, Norway, and sycamore are different types of:
   A. pine trees
   B. maple trees
   C. birch trees
   D. oak trees

4. The most common injuries resulting from the improper use of chain saws are injuries to the:
   A. face, head, and neck
   B. upper leg
   C. lower arm
   D. fingers and hand

5. All chain saw engines are:
    A. 2-cycle, air-cooled
    B. 4-cycle, air-cooled
    C. 2-cycle, water-cooled
    D. any of the above

6. Silviculture is:
    A. a compound used to repair damaged tree trunks
    B. a word meaning to "take care of forests"
    C. a word meaning "to trim forest lands"
    D. a method of planting trees for harvest

7. Factors which determine the fire susceptibility of a partic-
    ular forest area and the extent of a fire spreading are the
    moisture content of the trees and surrounding vegetation,
    atmospheric temperature, relative wind and humidity,
    and:
    A. the height of the trees
    B. the types of trees
    C. the arrangement of the trees
    D. the forest proximity to flat lands and clearings

8. Coniferous forests burn more readily than broad-leaved
    forests.
    True   False

9. Chain tension on a chain saw is correct when:
    A. You cannot lift the chain off the guide bar.
    B. You can lift the chain about ⅛ inch off the guide bar.
    C. The adjusting screw is turned in as far as it can go.
    D. The adjusting screw is turned out as far as it can go.

10. Tree scale sticks are used:
    A. to measure the exact location a tree will fall when it's
       chopped down
    B. to remove the bark from a tree
    C. to determine the tree's diameter and height
    D. to provide footing when scaling a tree

11. The correct ratio of oil-gasoline for most chain saws is:
    A. 2-to-1
    B. 5-to-1
    C. 30-to-1
    D. 50-to-1

12. Prior to replacing the spark plug on chain saws and brush cutters, the gap should be adjusted using:
    A. a matchbook cover
    B. a wire or flat gauge
    C. a ruler
    D. a tape measure

13. Bucking means:
    A. jumping up and down on a log to dislodge it
    B. scraping the bark off a tree with an axe
    C. cutting a tree into shorter lengths
    D. straddling a tree for ease of cutting

14. A full cord of wood measures:
    A. 6 feet by 6 feet by 6 feet
    B. 4 feet by 6 feet by 4 feet
    C. 8 feet by 8 feet by 8 feet
    D. 4 feet by 4 feet by 8 feet

15. For safety purposes, it's a good idea to:
    A. always debranch a tree after it has been felled
    B. limit debranching to a height no higher than your shoulder
    C. plant both feet firmly when cutting limbs that are over your head
    D. stand on a ladder when debranching high limbs

16. Scandinavian face cuts differ from traditional face cuts in:
    A. the height of the cut on the tree trunk
    B. the length of the backcut and the distance from the ground
    C. the degree of the cut
    D. all of the above

☆ T H E ☆
PALM READER
Test

Palmistry, or chiromancy, is a system of divination in which the structure of the hand is interpreted as being associated with the psychology and future of the individual. The practice dates back to China as early as 2000 B.C., and in Greek writings it was a well-known method of determining one's fate and future.

1. The kind of palmistry where the palmist describes the personality of the subject and points out the subject's good and bad qualities is called:
    A. divinatory palmistry
    B. psychotherapeutic palmistry
    C. holistic palmistry
    D. judgment palmistry

2. The kind of palmistry where the palmist matches the subject's hand with his or her physical and mental state as it applies to their health is called:
    A. divinatory palmistry
    B. holistic palmistry
    C. therapeutic palmistry
    D. blank palmistry

3. A reading from just one hand does not give a true picture of the subject.
    True   False

4. You can get a reasonably accurate interpretation of your
    subject using a palm print on paper taken with ink and a
    roller.
    True   False

5. A subject offering a relaxed hand with fingers slightly
    apart is some indication that he/she is:
    A. practical with wide interests and confident
    B. frustrated with a lot of self-reliance
    C. a good leader but stingy
    D. friendly and trusting
    E. Both A and D are correct.

6. The Mount of Venus is associated with:
    A. ignorance and good fortune
    B. knowledge and good conduct
    C. charity and love
    D. aggressiveness and anger

7. The Mount of Jupiter is associated with:
    A. religion and pride
    B. failure and obscurity
    C. laziness and dishonesty
    D. aptitude and aggressiveness

8. The length of the Life Line indicates the number of years
    of life. The longer the line, the longer your life. On your
    right hand, this line is located in the palm:
    A. to the left of the thumb near the Mount of Venus,
        running in a semi-circle
    B. underneath the pinky to the right of the second phalanx
    C. directly in the center of the palm to the left of the
        line of the liver
    D. in the center of the hand right of the Ring of Venus,
        running up and down

9. The Mount of the Moon is associated with:
    A. charity and wisdom
    B. knowledge and aptitude

    C. sensitivity and good conduct
    D. tenderness and love

10. If the end of the Life Line is forked, it means:
    A. the subject may have a change of life somewhere around the forked point
    B. the subject will inherit money somewhere around the forked point
    C. the subject may have a feeble old age
    D. the subject may experience a tragedy somewhere around the forked point

11. Most palmists suggest you should read the subject's left palm because it has the inherited traits.
    True   False

Most palmists agree that the shape of the fingers is some indication of the subject's personality and likes and dislikes.

12. Long, thin fingers are some indication the subject:
    A. is refined with an interest in information and solutions
    B. tends to make rash judgments based on only a few facts
    C. is delicate and upset by unplanned events
    D. is likely to choose a particular style of dress for the purpose of impressing friends

13. Short, fat fingers are some indication the subject:
    A. was destined to be a manual laborer despite other career goals
    B. is nervous
    C. is subject to violence
    D. is selfish and often irrational

14. The palm is divided into:
    A. four major sections
    B. five major sections
    C. nine major sections
    D. twelve major sections based on the Zodiac

★ T H E ★
MOTORCYCLIST
Test

1. The best way to help others see your motorcycle in the daytime is to:
   A. wear a white helmet
   B. ride in the left portion of the lane
   C. keep your headlight turned on

2. When adjusting your mirrors to carry a passenger, the passenger should:
   A. sit on the seat with you
   B. stand beside the cycle in the area covered by the motorcycle
   C. stand behind the cycle in the area covered by the mirrors

3. Before changing lanes to the left, you should:
   A. check the left mirror, then turn your head left
   B. check the right mirror, then the left mirror
   C. check the left mirror, then the right mirror

4. When making a turn at high speed, you should lean:
   A. more than you would at low speed
   B. less than you would at low speed
   C. the same amount as you would at low speed

5. Most motorcycle accidents occur:
   A. on interstate highways

B. on country roads
C. at intersections

6. To make a normal stop, you should use:
    A. the rear brake only
    B. the rear brake and downshift
    C. both front and rear brakes

7. When riding where sand and gravel have collected on paved roads, you should:
    A. avoid sudden changes in speed or direction
    B. downshift for more power
    C. slow down by using the rear brake only

8. When the front tire goes flat:
    A. the steering will feel jerky
    B. the cycle will tend to jerk from side to side
    C. the handlebars will shake violently

9. At intersections, the most common cause of motorcycle/car accidents is:
    A. the driver did not see the rider
    B. the rider was tailgating the driver
    C. the driver was tailgating the rider

10. To stop quickly in a turn, you should use:
    A. the rear brake only
    B. the front brake only
    C. both front and rear brakes

11. A motorcycle needs more frequent inspection and maintenance than a car because:
    A. It has more moving parts and cables.
    B. The engine is exposed to the weather.
    C. A breakdown is more likely to cause an accident.

12. To handle a slippery surface, you should:
    A. slow down before reaching it
    B. downshift when you reach it
    C. use the rear brake lightly while crossing

13. When the motorcycle is stopped, the passenger should:
     A. place both feet on the ground
     B. place the same foot on the ground that the operator
         does
     C. keep both feet on the footpegs

14. When the rear tire goes flat:
     A. The steering will feel heavy.
     B. The back of the cycle will jerk from side to side.
     C. You will lose power to the rear wheel.

15. At night, the equipment that makes it easiest for drivers
     following you to see is:
     A. a reflective vest
     B. light colored clothing
     C. a white helmet

16. When riding over a pothole, you should:
     A. keep normal seat position
     B. rise slightly off the seat
     C. lean forward as much as possible

17. When riding in traffic at night, the best way to locate
     bumps in the road is to:
     A. put your headlight on high beam
     B. watch the taillights of the car ahead
     C. read the road signs

18. Compared to cars, how much room do motorcycles usual-
     ly need to stop?
     A. barely one-half the distance
     B. about three-quarters of the distance
     C. at least as much distance

☆ T H E ☆
GOURMET CHEF
Test

Gourmet chefs, or cuisiniers, know what to do with food without consulting a cookbook. They understand recipes and techniques so well that with a simple list of ingredients they can produce a dish fit to set before a king. Cuisiniers carry this culinary information in their heads and the sight of a newly-caught salmon will prompt them to think of fifty or more ways to prepare it. They ask, "should we create a coulibiac or, perhaps, a mayonnaise de saumon?"

No cooking technique, from grilling to braising to poaching, is foreign to cuisiniers, and their manual dexterity is admirable. Cucumbers are transformed into fragile rounds as the chefs' knives fly and most chefs can crack two eggs simultaneously without breaking a single yolk. The cuisinier is at home in the medium of food and culinary language as an artist is with his paints and canvas.

1. Which of the following are considered to be the two most expensive spices?
    A. saffron and cardamon
    B. saffron and nutmeg
    C. nutmeg and mace
    D. cinnamon and coriander

2. Which of the following spices possesses the combined flavor of nutmeg, cinnamon, and clove?

    A. pumpkin pie spice
    B. anise
    C. allspice
    D. none of the above

3. A galantine is:
    A. a 128-ounce measuring vessel
    B. a colorful blend of diced vegetables
    C. a type of forcemeat
    D. a special breed of duck

4. The father of modern classical cuisine is:
    A. James Beard
    B. Auguste Escoffier
    C. Paul Prudomme
    D. Michel LeBorgne

5. Crème Anglaise is:
    A. put in French coffee
    B. a light custard sauce
    C. the base for some ice creams
    D. both B and C

6. Roast meat should be carved:
    A. immediately after cooking
    B. after a 10-minute rest
    C. after a 30-minute rest
    D. after an hour rest

7. Nesselrode is the name given to various cooked dishes and pastries containing:
    A. milk chocolate
    B. braised sweetbreads
    C. chestnut puree
    D. almond paste

8. The mixture known as "fine herbs" contains:
    A. parsley, chervil, tarragon, and chives
    B. rosemary, thyme, and garlic

C. parsley, garlic, and olive oil
D. celery, carrots, and onions

9. Cantal and cheddar are examples of:
   A. fresh unripened cheese
   B. goat's milk cheese
   C. pressed cow's milk cheese
   D. regions in northern England

10. A "bouquet garni" is used:
    A. to flavor a sauce or stock
    B. as a centerpiece
    C. to tenderize a roast
    D. none of the above

11. The main difference between braising and roasting is:
    A. Braising is done under a broiler while roasting is done in the oven.
    B. Braising is done in a closed vessel with very little liquid while roasting is done in an uncovered vessel with no liquid.
    C. Braising is done at high temperature, roasting is done at a low oven temperature.
    D. Braising is only used for whole fowl while roasting refers to any cut of meat.

12. The difference between Hollandaise and Bearnaise sauce is the addition of:
    A. parsley
    B. tarragon
    C. basil
    D. tomato

13. The highest grade of beef sold in the United States is:
    A. USDA Extra Fancy
    B. USDA Prime
    C. USDA Select
    D. FDA Premium

14. It is acceptable to add tomatoes when making brown stock.
    True   False

15. Hot stock should be placed immediately in the refrigerator to cool.
    True   False

16. Black butter, or beurre noir, is clarified butter heated until black in color.
    True   False

17. Bisque was traditionally thickened with rice.
    True   False

18. Oil is a better cooking medium than water because of its conductivity.
    True   False

19. Tomatoes cause green vegetables to turn a drab olive color.
    True   False

20. Hollandaise, Bearnaise, and Paloise all begin with an egg-butter emulsion.
    True   False

☆ THE ☆
CASINO PIT BOSS
Test

The pit boss at casinos in Las Vegas and Atlantic City is directly responsible for all activities in assigned pits. This includes taking care of game procedures, compliance to state and casino rules, insuring all equipment is operating properly, overseeing security, and supervision of all staff assigned to the work areas. Most of the casinos require pit bosses to be a high school graduate and hold a pit boss license from the state.

One of the major responsibilities is overseeing the games and insuring all rules are followed to the letter. The following questions pertain to the rules of the games at casinos in the United States.

1. In baccarat, the game is played with eight decks of cards. The object is to get a point count closest to nine. Picture cards and tens and any combination of cards totaling ten have no value. All other cards are counted at face value. A "natural" in baccarat is:
    A. a count of seven, eight, or nine
    B. a count of eight or nine
    C. a count higher than the dealer's count
    D. a total count of under ten with only two cards

2. The chances of rolling a seven on any given roll in craps is:
    A. 5 chances in 10

    B. 6 chances in 36
    C. 8 chances in 30
    D. even

3. The maximum number of players playing against the dealer in blackjack is usually:
    A. 4
    B. 7
    C. 9
    D. 12

4. Burying the top card after shuffling in the game of blackjack is called:
    A. burning
    B. tucking
    C. folding
    D. a slide

5. In the game of blackjack, a player holds a hand with an ace that he's counting as an 11 (instead of a one). That hand is known as a:
    A. a hard hand
    B. a soft hand
    C. a sucker's hand
    D. an edge hand

6. In the game of blackjack, the dealer must:
    A. hit on 16, stand on 17
    B. stand on 16, hit on 17
    C. hit on all cards under 21
    D. stand on all cards lower than the player to his left

7. The standard roulette wheel has:
    A. 36 numbered slots including the 0 and 00
    B. 37 numbered slots including the 0 and 00
    C. 38 numbered slots including the 0 and 00
    D. 40 numbered slots, not including the 0 and 00

8. In most European casinos, the roulette wheel differs from wheels in U.S. casinos by:

A. the number of 0 and 00 numbered slots
B. the arrangement of the numbers from 1 to 18
C. the colors for odd and even numbers
D. Both A and C are correct

9. The payoff bets on the roulette wheel are:
   A. 6-to-1 on a five-number split bet
   B. 10-to-1 on any one of two numbers
   C. 1-to-1 for any single number
   D. 8-to-2 for any column bet

10. In the game of seven-card stud:
    A. there is one card dealt face down
    B. there are two cards dealt face down
    C. all cards are dealt face down
    D. only the cards the player indicates are dealt face down

11. In the game of draw poker, a high-low draw means:
    A. The player with the lowest card gets to draw first.
    B. The player with the highest card gets to draw first.
    C. The pot is split between the lowest and highest hands.
    D. The dealer automatically wins if the player holding the
       highest hand and the player holding the lowest hand
       have similar cards.

12. In the game of roulette, the odds on color bets (red or
    black) are:
    A. even
    B. 2-to-1
    C. 4-to-1
    D. 5-to-1

13. The advantage the casino has over the player in the game
    of roulette is about:
    A. 1.25%
    B. 5.25%
    C. 10%
    D. 20%

☆ T H E ☆
SENATE PAGE
Test

Senate pages in Washington, D.C., are used primarily to deliver correspondence and legislative material within the congressional complex. Other duties include taking messages for members, calling them to the phone, preparing the chamber for Senate sessions, and carrying bills and amendments to the desk. A rotation system is used so that every page has an opportunity to experience the various areas of service.

The United States Senate Page School provides accredited academic instruction and eligibility is limited to juniors in high school. Pages are paid on the basis of an annual salary of $9,090 or $757 a month. Pages reside at the United States House of Representative's Page Residence Hall and the cost of residency, including meals, is $300 a month.

1. Under the American system of government, individuals have various rights which are stated in the Constitution, including the 24 amendments, and as developed, extended, and elaborated by judicial decisions. Which of the following do you consider to be the most inclusive statement of the nature of these rights?

   A. No provisions whatever regarding civil rights and liberties of individuals are provided in the original Constitution; all provisions of this nature have been included by adoption of amendments.

   B. Numerous restrictions on both the national and state

governments are established by the first ten amendments to the Constitution.

C. These guarantees generally give protection to individuals against various kinds of action by the national government as well as against various kinds of action by state and local government.

D. Emphasis is placed on the right of adult men and women to vote without restrictions other than age and citizenship.

2. In which respect does the post of the speaker of the House of Representatives of the United States most closely resemble that of the speaker of the British House of Commons?

A. Both must be members of the majority party in power during their terms as speakers.

B. Both may speak in debate and vote on pending legislation.

C. Both are impartial in their rulings and interpretations of legislative rules and procedures.

D. Both are elected to their respective legislative bodies by their constituencies.

3. Which of the following statements correctly describes the status of the presidential primary in the United States?

A. Only a minority of states has presidential primaries.

B. More states use presidential primaries than state conventions.

C. Only 40 states have presidential primaries.

D. The number of states having presidential primaries has steadily increased in the last 50 years.

4. Though the president sometimes calls the Senate into special session without calling the House of Representatives, he never calls the House of Representatives into special sessions without at the same time calling the Senate because:

A. The House of Representatives is too unwieldy a body and too widely scattered geographically to make a special session of that group alone profitable from a legislative point of view.

B. The Constitution specifically prohibits his calling of special sessions of the House of Representatives alone.

C. Special Sessions of the Senate alone are generally called either for the purpose of ratifying treaties or confirming appointments.

D. No president has dared to offend the Senate by calling only the House into special session.

5. In order to expedite the legislative process, the House of Representatives:

A. requires debates to be continued until a topic is disposed of

B. authorizes the speaker to determine that a quorum exists by counting as present all members actually in the chamber

C. considers measures in order of their appearance from committee rooms

D. relegates all minor issues to be given consideration on particular days

6. American political parties perform the functions of:

1. recruiting candidates and staffing government
2. bridging the gap created by separation of powers
3. simplifying and organizing political viewpoints
4. unifying the nation and integrating various points of view within the electorate

A. All of the above are correct.

B. Only 1 and 3 above are correct.

C. Only 3 above is correct.

D. Only 1, 2, and 4 above are correct.

7. "Folkways of the United States Senate" refers to:

A. meeting the demands of the folks back home in a senator's home state

B. personal characteristic of senators which distinguish them from other congressmen

C. rules such as the filibuster and seniority which uniquely characterize this body

D. informal expectations that senators have of their colleagues

8. The Constitution of the United States prohibits states from:
   1. coining money
   2. passing bills of attainder or ex post facto laws
   3. making gold and silver coin legal tender
   4. granting letters of marque and reprisal
   A. Only 1, 2, and 3 above are correct.
   B. All of the above are correct.
   C. Only 1, 2, and 4 above are correct.
   D. Only 2, 3, and 4 above are correct.

9. Which of the following statements concerning United States citizenship is not true?
   A. The term "citizens of the United States" is defined in the Fourteenth Amendment.
   B. Chinese admitted to the United States may acquire citizenship by naturalization.
   C. All aliens must reside here for a minimum of five years before being qualified as to residency for citizenship.
   D. An American woman retains her citizenship even though she marries an alien.

☆ THE ☆
WINE CONNOISSEUR
Test

A wine connoisseur is someone who likes history and culture, science and gardening, and taste and flavor. A knowledgeable wine aficionado is someone who knows that the appreciation of wine alone is one thing but that its evaluation with food is something else—a lifetime of discovery and surprise.

1. Which of the following countries has the world's northern-most vineyards?
    A. Russia
    B. Germany
    C. Luxembourg
    D. Belgium
    E. Nova Scotia

2. Which of the following regions in France is responsible for initiating the Appellation d'Origine Controle system?
    A. Alsace
    B. Bordeaux
    C. Côte Du Rhone
    D. Burgundy
    E. Armagnac

3. Every year is a vintage year.
    True   False

4. When choosing a red wine with fish, make sure it is light and fruity.
   True   False

5. Which of the following is the smallest red wine-producing commune in Bordeaux?
   A. St. Julien
   B. Graves
   C. Listrac
   D. Pomerol
   E. Pauillac

6. Which of the following nations produces the highest volume of wine?
   A. Spain
   B. U.S.A.
   C. France
   D. Italy
   E. Australia

7. Sherry is a fortified wine that stimulates pancreatic secretions.
   True   False

8. The first U.S. winery was located in:
   A. Virginia
   B. Missouri
   C. California
   D. New York
   E. Florida

9. A rheoboam holds how many 750 ml. bottles?
   A. 7
   B. 4
   C. 6
   D. 8
   E. 10

10. Carbonic maceration describes the technique of adding

carbon dioxide gas to a finished wine in order to make it sparkle.
True   False

11. Wine is a low calorie, nutritious beverage.
True   False

12. Vintage port is distinguished by the time it ages in the cask.
True   False

13. Chapitalization, the process of adding sugar to the must, is used to make the world's great sweet wines.
True   False

14. Wine kept in small containers ages slower than wines kept in large containers.
True   False

15. Lactic acid is most palatable to humans.
True   False

16. An acidic white wine would be a bad choice for a dinner featuring fatty sausage.
True   False

17. Which of the following grapes is not a member of the *Vitis vinifera* family?
A. Barbera
B. Chenin Blanc
C. Malvasia
D. De Chaunac
E. Ruby Cabernet

☆ T H E ☆
LACK OF KNOWLEDGE
Test

The purpose of this test is to illustrate that much of what we know—or think we know—may not be valid.

Some of the questions on this test are fairly straightforward while others serve to illustrate a lack of knowledge in areas in which most people assume they are not totally ignorant. This test was prepared by John B. Means, executive director of the National Association of Self-Instructional Language Programs at Temple University.

1. The largest American city with a woman as a mayor is:
   A. Indianapolis
   B. Kansas City
   C. Seattle
   D. Houston
   E. San Francisco

2. The capital city closest to the geographical center of its state is the capital city of:
   A. Colorado
   B. Iowa
   C. Arkansas
   D. New Jersey
   E. Ohio

3. The state capitol building closest to its neighboring state is in:

    A. Rhode Island
    B. New Jersey
    C. New Hampshire
    D. Delaware
    E. Kentucky

4. The state with the smallest population in its capital city is:
    A. Alaska
    B. Vermont
    C. Delaware
    D. South Dakota
    E. New Hampshire

Match the most widely-spoken language in Column B with the continent in Column A:

5. North America	A. Mandarin Chinese
6. South America	B. English
7. Europe	C. Arabic
8. Asia	D. Russian
9. Africa	E. Portuguese

List the largest countries in geographical area for each of the locations listed below:

10. North America   _____
11. South America   _____
12. Europe   _____
13. Asia   _____
14. Africa   _____

List the largest city in population for each of the countries listed in below.

15. Brazil   _____
16. The People's Republic
    of China   _____
17. Scotland   _____
18. India   _____
19. Switzerland   _____

List the largest island in the locations below:

20. The Atlantic Ocean   _____
21. The Indian Ocean   _____
22. The Pacific Ocean   _____
23. The Mediterranean Sea   _____
24. The Caribbean Sea   _____

25. Which of the states listed below each border on eight other states?
    A. Kentucky and Virginia
    B. Colorado and Idaho
    C. Tennessee and Missouri
    D. Iowa and Kansas
    E. California and Nevada

26. Which of the following nations is considered one of the most urban in the world because of its lack of rural areas?
    A. The Netherlands
    B. Singapore
    C. Bangladesh
    D. Japan
    E. Belgium

27. Which of the following states has the highest population density?
    A. New Jersey
    B. New York
    C. Rhode Island
    D. California
    E. Massachusetts

Match the presidents listed in Column with their birthplaces in Column B.

28.	Tyler	A.	Illinois
29.	Lincoln	B.	Massachusetts
30.	Hoover	C.	Texas
31.	Eisenhower	D.	Virginia
32.	Reagan	E.	Kentucky
33.	Bush	F.	Iowa

☆ T H E ☆
PSYCHIATRIC NURSE
Test

1. Which of the following best describes how the nurse should deal with manic patients?
   A. with enthusiasm
   B. with encouraging support
   C. with understanding
   D. with quiet calmness
   E. with a reassuring manner that reduces anxiety

2. What is the most prominent symptom of senile dementia?
   A. an impaired time sense
   B. disorientation
   C. difficulty with abstract reasoning
   D. impairment in the ability to retain and recall information
   E. difficulty in identifying people

3. Which of the following statements is most appropriate to a delusional patient who fearfully explains people are waiting outside to kill him?
   A. "You don't have to worry because you are safe here."
   B. "You know as well as I do that no one is trying to kill you."
   C. "You should rest now and when you wake up I'm certain you'll feel less afraid."
   D. "You should go to occupational therapy to take your mind off your fears."
   E. "I understand how frightened you feel but when you're better, you'll see things in a different way."

4. When the primary patient does not or cannot verbalize for himself during a family conference, the nurse should:
   A. urge the patient to talk
   B. allow other family members to talk for the patient
   C. accept the patient's silence
   D. support the patient by expressing her own feelings when they correspond with the patient's
   E. allow the patient to return to the ward

5. In certain periods of development, anti-social behavior in young children is considered normal. However, of the following situations, the one which merits referral to a mental health professional is where:
   A. A two-year-old persists in hitting his four-year-old brother.
   B. A three-year-old develops enuresis when a new baby is brought into the house.
   C. A four-year-old runs away from home at every opportunity.
   D. A six-year-old is not friendly, has no friends after six months in school, and participates in activities only when compelled to.

6. Why is each member of a family given a screening interview prior to family therapy treatment?
   A. to determine the nature of the problem
   B. to construct a program of therapy
   C. to collect data relevant to the treatment of the primary patient
   D. to determine whether the problem can be treated and whether the family is willing to commit its members to treatment
   E. to determine which member should be hospitalized

7. What should the nurse's reaction be to a manic patient's loud jokes and crude pranks?
   A. studied prudishness
   B. acknowledgement with hilarity
   C. restraints on the patient

   D. with silence, ignoring the behavior
   E. chastise the patient

8. Who of the following is least likely to make a suicide
   attempt?
   A. the patient with a history of suicide attempts
   B. members of the patient's family who have a history of
      suicide attempts
   C. patients who obsessively fear that they will commit
      suicide
   D. patients who write suicide notes
   E. patients who have access to suicidal agents

9. Which of the following are qualities that distinguish the
   schizophrenic from the non-schizophrenic?
   1. a diminished capacity to experience pleasure
   2. a strong tendency to be dependent on others
   3. an awareness that there is a disturbance in mental
      functioning
   4. a noteworthy impairment in social competence
   5. partial loss of adaption
   A. 1, 2, and 3 are correct
   B. 1, 2, and 4 are correct
   C. 1, 4, and 5 are correct
   D. 1, 2, and 5 are correct
   E. 2, 3, and 4 are correct

10. From our knowledge about hallucinatory phenomena, it
    can be stated reliably that:
    A. Hallucinations occur in association with a dream-like
       state.
    B. Hallucinations and imagery are similar processes differing
       only in intensity.
    C. Mescal-induced hallucinations are not similar to schiz-
       ophrenic hallucinations.
    D. Organized hallucinations can be produced by direct
       stimulation of the brain surface.

☆ THE ☆
POLICE OFFICER
Test

1. The primary reason for the police to try to find out which make, model, and year of car was involved in the commission of a crime is to:
   A. compare the tire tracks left at the scene of the crime with the tires used on cars of that make
   B. determine if the mud on the tires of the suspected car matches the mud on the unpaved road near the scene of the crime
   C. reduce to a large extent the amount of work involved in determining the particular car used in the commission of the crime
   D. alert the police patrol forces to question the occupants of all automobiles of that type

2. While on duty, an officer observes a person standing on a tenth-floor window sill threatening to jump. The best action for the officer to take first is to:
   A. phone his supervisor for additional officers and proper rescue equipment
   B. go to the tenth floor, get as close as possible to the person, and urge him not to jump
   C. attempt to locate relatives or friends of the person and ask their immediate assistance
   D. stop all traffic on the street and have all parked cars removed from the side near the building

3. While a clerk in a shoe store is making change following the sale of a pair of shoes to a man, the man takes a pistol out of his pocket and orders the clerk to hand over the money in the cash register. Of the following facts later given to the police by the clerk, the one most useful in attempting to apprehend the criminal is that he had:
   A. a Z-shaped scar over his left ankle
   B. a constant twitch on the left side of his face
   C. a mustache and long sideburns
   D. purchased size 7DDD blue suede shoes

4. While on duty at the scene of a strike, an officer is ordered to assist in the dispersal of an unruly mob that has already destroyed much valuable property. The police have the mob moving in the right direction and are breaking the group into several smaller groups. The offi cer, while taking part in this action, passes several strikers lying on the ground and bleeding from apparently minor and superficial injuries. Of the following, the action the officer should take is to:
   A. continue dispersing the mob and not stop to render first aid to the injured strikers
   B. discontinue dispersing the mob and not stop to render first aid to the injured strikers
   C. continue dispersing the mob but allow as many strik ers as wish to do so to remain with the injured
   D. discontinue dispersing the mob in order to determine the seriousness of the injuries

5. After stopping a motorist who has just committed a traffic violation, an officer asks the motorist for his operator's license. The motorist hands the officer his wallet and says that his license is in the wallet. The officer should not accept the wallet mainly:
   A. because the sorting of papers and cards contained in the wallet would be too time consuming for the officer
   B. to discourage the motorist from any possible bribery offer

    C. to lessen the possibility that the motorist will later claim that money or papers were taken from the wallet

    D. to minimize the temptation for the officer to look at papers and cards of a personal nature

6. An apparently disturbed man, waving his arms wildly and muttering incoherently, approaches an officer on a busy street. When questioned several times by the officer, he makes no response but continues his behavior. The best of the following actions for the officer to take first is to:

    A. keep the man with him and telephone headquarters for assistance

    B. isolate the man by taking him into a hallway or uncrowded store

    C. warn the man to behave or face possible arrest for disturbing the police

    D. place the man in a horizontal position and treat him for shock

7. An officer is asked by a citizen the location of a candy store which the officer knows is under observation for suspected bookmaking activities. In such a situation, the officer should:

    A. give the proper directions to the citizen

    B. give the proper directions to the citizen but tell him the store is under observation

    C. state that he does not know the location of the store

    D. tell the citizen that he may be arrested if the store is raided

Many factors must be considered when a police officer is deciding whether or not to make an arrest. If an arrest is not considered legal, it could mean that some evidence will not be allowed in court. At other times, an arrest may tip off a suspect before evidence can be found. In all cases, an arrest takes away from a person the very important right of liberty. It is very upsetting to a person and it causes worry and possibly the loss of money. On the other hand, the officer must also realize that if an arrest is delayed too long, the suspect may run away or the evidence might be destroyed.

On the basis of the information in the paragraph above:

8. A judge may refuse to accept evidence of a crime if:
   A. It interfered with the suspect's rights to liberty.
   B. It was found after the suspect was tipped off.
   C. The suspect was able to get away.
   D. It was collected during an illegal arrest.

On the basis of the information in the paragraph above:

9. In deciding whether to make an arrest, a police officer should:
   A. consider whether the suspect is a known criminal
   B. realize that an innocent person could be very upset by being arrested
   C. not delay since evidence can be found later
   D. not worry about the innocent person because the courts will free him

10. A police officer chases a suspected burglar down a street which is crowded with people and cars. Suddenly the suspect turns and fires, narrowly missing the officer. The officer should:
    A. continue the chase with caution
    B. stop the chase before someone gets hurt
    C. shoot back before the suspect gets away
    D. fire a warning shot over the suspect's head

11. During a riot, it is the practice of the police to take the leaders into custody as soon as possible. Of the following, the most valid reason for doing this is to:
    A. arrest suspects in the order of their importance
    B. remove the leaders from the scene so that the rioting may cease sooner
    C. punish the leaders more than other rioters, which is fair since they started the riot
    D. obtain valuable information from the leaders

☆ THE ☆
MEDICAL DIAGNOSTICIAN
Test

1. One sign of hypertension is:
   A. a blood pressure reading of 140/98
   B. a blood pressure reading of 118/70
   C. elevated blood sugar
   D. a temperature of 103 degrees F. or higher

2. Fever, headache, nausea, and patches of yellow membrane forming in the throat and growing into one large membrane that could interfere with swallowing and breathing is one indication of:
   A. strep throat
   B. diphtheria
   C. typhoid fever
   D. malaria

3. The symptoms of gout are:
   A. a stiff neck
   B. swelling of the lymph nodes
   C. pain in the joints
   D. sore throat and fever

4. A hiatus hernia is located in:
   A. the intestine
   B. the heart and lungs
   C. the esophagus and stomach
   D. the brain

Match the medical terms in Column A with the correct descriptions in Column B.

	A		**B**
5.	trauma	A.	broken bone
6.	edema	B.	memory loss
7.	fever	C.	elevated temperature
8.	fracture	D.	infection
9.	amnesia	E.	ringing in the ears
10.	inflammation	F.	dizziness
11.	urticaria	G.	swelling
12.	tinnitus	H.	injury
13.	vertigo	I.	heart attack
14.	myocardial infarction	J.	itching of the skin

15. Seeing frequent flashes of light and showers of drifting black spots are symptomatic of:
    A. a detached retina
    B. a migraine headache
    C. a stroke
    D. high blood pressure

16. When inflamed, the prostate gland will produce which of the following symptoms?
    A. difficulty in urinating
    B. a change in urinary stream
    C. lower back pain
    D. all of the above

17. The 140 in a blood pressure reading of 140/70 is the:
    A. diastolic pressure
    B. systolic pressure
    C. the same as the patient's pulse rate
    D. number of heart beats every 15 seconds

18. Bell's palsy is paralysis of the:
    A. lower leg nerves
    B. chest muscle nerves
    C. facial muscles nerves
    D. fingers

19. Angina pectoris means chest pain.
    True   False

20. The Islands of Langerhans are located in the:
    A. gall bladder
    B. pancreas
    C. liver
    D. brain

21. A joint mouse is:
    A. a free floating bone fragment in a joint
    B. a high sound in the heart
    C. a tumor in the abdomen
    D. water in the ear

22. Strabismus affects:
    A. the ears
    B. the lungs
    C. the eyes
    D. the joints

23. Bile is produced in:
    A. the liver
    B. the gall bladder
    C. the kidney
    D. the large intestine

☆ ANSWERS ☆

Answers—**The Weatherman Test**

1. C
2. A
3. C
4. D
5. D
6. A
7. True. The critical factor in determining the major sky color is the size of scattered particles that normally create a red color. On rare occasions, these particles are just the right size to scatter the red-making component of moonlight and make the moon appear to be blue.
8. B
9. B
10. True
11. D
12. B
13. False. The air is cooled by water vapor, not heated.
14. C
15. False. Radiation fog is a nighttime phenomenon occurring when the wind is light, the humidity is high and the sky is clear.
16. B
17. A

Answers—**The District Attorney Test**   ☆

1. A	**6.** A
2. D	**7.** A
3. A	**8.** C
4. C	**9.** A
5. D	**10.** E

Answers—**The Football Referee Test**   ☆

1. B	**8.** B
2. A	**9.** C
3. D	**10.** E
4. D	**11.** A
5. B	**12.** C
6. B	**13.** C
7. A	**14.** A

Answers—**The Nanny Test**   ☆

1. C	**8.** D
2. B	**9.** B
3. B	**10.** A
4. B	**11.** A
5. C	**12.** D
6. C	**13.** C
7. B	

Answers—**The Army Cook Test**   ☆

1. D	**5.** B
2. A	**6.** A
3. C	**7.** D
4. C	**8.** C

9. D	**12.** A
10. D	**13.** A
11. D	**14.** C

Answers—**The Quiz Show Test**   ☆

1. What are the Virgin Islands?
2. What are the Aleutian Islands?
3. What is Greenland?
4. What are the Channel Islands?
5. What are the Philippine Islands?
6. What is Italy?
7. What is Idaho?
8. What is Iowa?
9. What is the Van Gogh painting "Irises?"
10. What is Iran?
11. What is intelligent or intellectual?
12. What is inhibited or introverted?
13. What is indecisive?
14. What is irresponsible or immature?
15. What is inspire?
16. Who is the governor of New York?
17. Who is the governor of California?
18. Who is the governor of Vermont?
19. Who is the governor of Hawaii?
20. Who is the governor of Illinois?
21. Who is Bob Hope?
22. Who is Ringo Starr?
23. Who is Joan Fontaine?
24. Who is Ronald Reagan?
25. Who is Michael Jackson?
26. How many Americans are living with someone else's heart?
27. What is a heart attack?
28. When and where was the first human heart transplant performed?
29. What is "My Heart Belongs To Daddy?"

30. What is Chevrolet's motto?
31. What is better and bettor?
32. What is a binocle and a binnacle?
33. What is bear and bare?
34. What is buoy and boy?
35. What is board and bored?
36. How many squares are there on a chess board?
37. How many chess pieces are there in a chess set?
38. Who makes the first move?
39. Who are U.S. Chess champions?
40. What is the World Chess Federation?
41. What is the deepest point in the Pacific Ocean (the Mariana Trench)?
42. What is the length of the Mississippi River?
43. What is a mnemonic or key word for remembering the Great Lakes—Huron, Ontario, Michigan, Erie and Superior?
44. What are the world's five largest bodies of water?
45. What are the upper and lower limits of the Rio Grande?
46. Who is Gene Hackman or director William Friedkin?
47. Who is John Voight or Jane Fonda?
48. Who is Dustin Hoffman or Meryl Streep?
49. Who is director David Lean?
50. Who is Liza Minnelli or director Bob Fosse?
51. Where is the Swimming Hall of Fame?
52. Where is the Baseball Hall of Fame?
53. Where is the Wrestling Hall of Fame?
54. Where is the Professional Rodeo Cowboy Hall of Fame?
55. Where is the Bowling Hall of Fame?

Answers—**The Shepherd Test**

1. B
2. C
3. A
4. B
5. C
6. C
7. B
8. D
9. False. The Old English Sheepdog is primarily a show dog and only a few have the ability to work
10. C
11. True
12. B
13. C
14. D
15. False. By blowing into its nostrils.
16. True

Answers—**The Criminal Investigator Test**

1. A
2. D
3. B
4. B
5. D
6. C
7. D
8. C
9. D
10. C
11. C
12. D
13. C

Answers—**The Ship's Officer and Deckhand Test**

1. B
2. A
3. A
4. A
5. A
6. B
7. B
8. C
9. B
10. B
11. C
12. B
13. B
14. A
15. B

Answers—**The Hospital Nutritionist Test**   ☆

1. True. Malnutrition means "bad nutrition" and obesity is
   one of the major forms of malnutrition in the United
   States. It is caused by the consumption of too many
   calories that are inefficiently utilized by the body and
   which, all too often, have little or no nutritional value.
2. True. There is no practical difference between the calories in butter, margarine, and cooking fat and the fat in
   your body. A pound of butter contains 3,500 calories, the
   equivalent of the calories in a pound of body fat.
3. False. You might have a tendency to inherit some brown
   fat but what you do inherit is bone structure, eating
   habits, and an attitude toward food.
4. False. Most quick weight-loss diets omit some important
   nutrients. You need the basic foods to maintain good
   health: dairy, meat, vegetables and fruits, and breads
   and cereals.
5. False. Pizza made with meat, cheese, and tomatoes
   contains worthwhile nutrients, so you're getting some
   protein, calcium, and iron and the A, C, and B complex
   vitamins.
6. A
7. True. Chemically, sugar cane and sugar from sugar beets
   are the same.
8. True
9. False
10. True. More starchy foods and sweets are consumed, not
    to mention the additional calories from alcoholic cock-
    tails that often accompany a restaurant meal
11. False. Vitamins are either water soluble or fat soluble.
    The water soluble vitamins are B and C; and any not
    needed is excreted from the body. Fat soluble vitamins
    like A and D are stored in the body and could be toxic if
    taken in excess.
12. B
13. C
14. C

15. C
16. C

Answers—**The Witch Test**   ☆

1. A	**7.** A
2. B	**8.** D
3. A	**9.** B
4. A	**10.** B
5. C	**11.** B
6. B	

Answers—**The Deep Sea Diver Test**   ☆

1. B	**10.** B
2. B	**11.** D
3. A	**12.** C
4. B	**13.** False. The air pressure increases and the water pressure decreases, causing the lungs to expand which could result in a ruptured lung.
5. C	
6. B	
7. C	
8. C	
9. False. Salt water is heavier and more buoyant than fresh water. In fresh water, you would use more weights than you would in salt water.	**14.** B
	15. C

Answers—**The Cultural Literacy Test**   ☆

1. A	**8.** B
2. D	**9.** C
3. A	**10.** A
4. A	**11.** D
5. B	**12.** C
6. D	**13.** D
7. B	**14.** B

15. B
16. A
17. 1-B
    2-E
    3-F

4-G
5-D
6-C
7-A

Answers—**The Bartender Test**   ☆

1. A
2. B
3. A
4. A
5. B
6. A
7. False
8. False

9. A
10. D
11. Planter's Punch
12. Singapore Sling
13. Poor Man's Bloody Mary
14. Grasshopper
15. Zombie

Answers—**The Chess Master Test**   ☆

1. C
2. B
3. B. A match was played between Baltimore and Washington, D.C., in 1844, the same year the telegraph was invented.
4. B. It was held in Madrid, Spain at the court of King Philip of Spain.
5. True. Although probably Persian or Indian in its origin, the first known historical document connected with chess is an inscription on a tablet found in a pyramid at Gizeh, dating back to 3000 B.C.
6. True. *The Game and Playe of Chesse* was published by Caxton's Press in 1474.
7. True. A spy overheard Washington's plan for crossing the Delaware and sent a note to the Hessian General Rawle. Engrossed in a game of chess, he put the notice in his vest pocket and went back to playing the game. When American soldiers searched his body the next day, they found the note...unread.

8. False

9. B. The game was played by Stepak and Mashian in Israel in 1980 and lasted 24½ hours.

10. C. Oscar Panno, unwilling to play the final round in Palma in 1980 and equally unwilling to forfeit, allowed Bobby Fischer to play 1.P-QB4, then promptly resigned.

11. True. The Roman Catholic Church banned the game in 1400. Islamic lawyers argued that the chess pieces represented figures of war. The U.S.S.R., noting the early death of Harry Nelson Pillsbury, a noted blindfold player, and perhaps overreacting to blindfold world record holder Alexander Alekhine's desertion, banned the play of blindfold chess in 1930.

12. C

13. C. Estimates are from 31,000,000 to over one billion.

14. A

15. C

16. B. J. Dobrusky scored 13-0-1 in the blindfold competition. In 1891, a match was played at the Manhattan Chess Club between bald-headed members and members with hair. The bald headed members won, 14 games to 11.

Answers—**The Miss America™ Contestant Test**   ☆

1. C	9. True
2. False	10. C
3. A	11. B
4. B	12. A
5. B	13. B
6. True	14. B
7. C	15. True
8. B	

Answers—**The Washington, D.C., Tour Guide Test**   ☆

1. C	5. B
2. C	6. C
3. C	7. A
4. D	8. C

9. B
10. A
11. C
12. B

13. A
14. C
15. C

Answers—**The Professional Golfer Test** ☆

1. B
2. B
3. A
4. A
5. B
6. B
7. C
8. A

9. B
10. B
11. C
12. B
13. A
14. B
15. B

Answers—**The Bomb Disposal Test** ☆

1. C
2. B
3. A
4. C
5. A
6. C
7. A
8. B

9. A
10. D
11. A
12. B
13. A
14. B
15. A
16. B

Answers—**The Chinese Cook Test** ☆

1. B
2. B
3. False. Both of these dishes are an American invention.
4. A
5. B

6. True
7. True
8. C
9. B
10. D
11. True
12. False

13. True
14. True
15. True
16. False
17. C

18. True
19. False
20. True
21. True

Answers—**The London Taxi Driver Test**   ☆

1. A
2. B
3. A
4. True
5. B
6. B
7. B

8. B
9. C
10. A
11. A
12. C
13. B

Answers—**The Know-It-All Test**   ☆

1. B
2. C
3. A
4. D
5. C
6. B
7. They were all born in New York City.
8. They were all born in 1944.
9. B
10. A
11. C
12. L
13. I
14. D
15. C
16. J
17. A
18. B

19. H
20. K
21. E
22. F
23. G
24. B
25. B
26. A
27. D
28. C
29. True. Swimming the breaststroke at 56 strokes a minute or rowing at 33 strokes a minute burns up about 1,200-1,400 calories an hour compared to only 660 calories an hour for bicycling.
30. D

Answers—**The Prison Guard Test**

1. C	**6D.** False
2. C	**6E.** True
3. A	**6F.** False
4. B	**6G.** False
5. D	**7.** C
6A. False	**8.** B
6B. False	**9.** C
6C. False	**10.** D

Answers—**The French Interpreter Test**

1. B	**9.** B
2. A	**10.** C
3. C	**11.** A
4. B	**12.** C
5. B	**13.** A
6. A	**14.** C
7. D	**15.** A
8. B	

Answers—**The Grandstand Contestant Test**

1. Maurice "Rocket" Richard
2. Soldier Field
3. Cruiserweight
4. Drew Pearson
5. Earl Wynn, Bob Lemon, Mike Garcia
6. The Milwaukee Brewers
7. The Kansas City-Omaha Kings
8. Pat O'Brien
9. Sandy Koufax
10. Craig Morton
11. Wilfred Benitez
12. Iowa
13. Griffith Stadium
14. Bobby Carpenter
15. John L. Sullivan
16. Andy Mill
17. The Miami Dolphins
18. Tom Watson
19. *Ring* magazine
20. Barbara Potter
21. Jo Jo White
22. Jack Dempsey
23. Tennessee
24. Carl Hubbell
25. *The Stars and Stripes*

Answers—**The Sexologist Test**   ☆

1. B   9. B
2. C   10. A
3. A   11. A
4. D   12. C
5. B   13. False
6. A   14. D
7. B   15. B
8. True. Based on national   16. D
   statistics, out of every   17. C
   1,000 divorced men 880
   will remarry while only
   752 women out of every
   1,000 divorced women
   will remarry.

Answers—**The Charter Boat Captain Test**   ☆

1. D   8. B
2. A   9. C
3. B   10. C
4. A   11. C
5. B   12. D
6. A   13. C
7. D

Answers—**The Boring Person Test**   ☆

If you have answered over 12 of these questions with "True,"
there's a good chance people think you're a boring person. If
you answer about eight with "True," you need to think about
being more active in terms of hobbies, participation in organi-
zations, career, and home life. If you answered most of the
questions with "False," the odds are you're too busy to be
bored or boring anyone else.

Answers—**The Psychic Test**

1. A and C
2. B and C
3. A. It's inexcusable to miss this one.
4. C
5. B and C
6. C
7. C. They've paid for companionship and sharing.
8. C. You never express an opinion. The client must have a desire to solve his problems before anything will really work. Your opinion means nothing.
9. C
10. B
11. C

Answers—**The Lumberjack Test**

1. A
2. C
3. B
4. D
5. A
6. B
7. C
8. True
9. B
10. C
11. C
12. B
13. C
14. D
15. A
16. C. Scandinavian face cuts are made at about 90 degrees while traditional face cuts are made at about 45 degrees

Answers—**The Palm Reader Test**

1. B
2. C
3. True. Most palmists prefer reading both hands, starting out with the left hand if you're right-handed, the right hand if you're left-handed.
4. True
5. A
6. C
7. A
8. A
9. C
10. C
11. True
12. A
13. D
14. C

Answers—**The Motorcyclist Test**

1. C	10. C
2. A	11. C
3. A	12. A
4. A	13. C
5. C	14. B
6. C	15. A
7. A	16. B
8. A	17. B
9. A	18. C

Answers—**The Gourmet Chef Test**

1. A	11. B
2. C	12. B
3. C	13. B
4. B	14. True
5. D	15. False
6. C	16. False
7. C	17. True
8. A	18. False
9. C	19. True
10. A	20. True

Answers—**The Casino Pit Boss Test**

1. B	8. A
2. B	9. A
3. B	10. B
4. A	11. C
5. B	12. A
6. A	13. B
7. C	

Answers—**The Senate Page Test**

1. C	3. A
2. D	4. C

5. B
6. A
7. D

8. C
9. C

Answers—**The Wine Connoisseur Test**

1. B
2. C
3. True
4. True
5. D
6. D
7. True
8. B
9. C
10. False. It's a fermentation technique for light, fruity red wines.
11. True

12. False. By the time it ages in the bottle.
13. False. It's used to increase the alcohol content.
14. False. Wine kept in small containers ages faster than wine kept in large containers.
15. True
16. False. It would be a good choice.
17. D

Answers—**The Lack of Knowledge Test**

1. D
2. D
3. B
4. B
5. B
6. E
7. D
8. A
9. C
10. Canada
11. Brazil
12. The U.S.S.R.
13. The U.S.S.R.
14. Sudan
15. Sao Paulo
16. Shanghai
17. Glasgow

18. Calcutta
19. Zurich
20. Greenland
21. Madagascar
22. New Guinea
23. Sicily
24. Cuba
25. C
26. B
27. A
28. D
29. E
30. F
31. C
32. A
33. B

Answers—**The Psychiatric Nurse Test** ☆

1. D
2. D
3. E
4. D
5. D
6. D
7. D
8. C
9. D
10. D

Answers—**The Police Officer Test** ☆

1. C
2. A
3. B
4. A
5. B
6. A
7. A
8. D
9. B
10. A
11. B

Answers—**The Medical Diagnostician Test** ☆

1. A
2. B
3. C
4. C
5. H
6. G
7. C
8. A
9. B
10. D
11. J
12. E
13. F
14. I
15. A
16. D
17. B
18. C
19. True
20. B
21. A
22. C
23. B

PHAROS BOOKS are available at special discounts on bulk purchases for sales promotions, premiums, fundraising, or educational use. For details, contact the Special Sales Department, Pharos Books, 200 Park Avenue, New York, NY 10166.